WINNER TAKE NOTHING

Ernest Hemingway ran across the roofs of two more buildings, then stopped. An alleyway, at least twelve feet wide, separated him from the next building.

He didn't want to jump across. The broad jump had never been his sport. He didn't feel like tripping and falling fifty feet to his death.

There was a sudden cracking sound and a piece of roof blew off near his feet. Five buildings away stood the two men, the one with the gun taking aim. Hemingway zigzagged back several feet. He heard another shot, felt nothing. Then he ran, pushing off the roof with all his strength.

He almost made it.

THE HEMINGWAY PAPERS
A Novel by
Vincent Cosgrove

BANTAM BOOKS
TORONTO · NEW YORK · LONDON · SYDNEY

Author's Note:
Though inspired by a true incident, *The Hemingway Papers* is a work of fiction.

THE HEMINGWAY PAPERS
A Bantam Book / October 1983

All rights reserved.
Copyright © 1983 by Vincent Cosgrove.
Cover art copyright © 1983 by Chet Jezierski.
This book may not be reproduced in whole or in part, by mimeograph or any other means, without permission.
For information address: Bantam Books, Inc.

ISBN 0-553-23580-X

Published simultaneously in the United States and Canada

Bantam Books are published by Bantam Books, Inc. Its trademark, consisting of the words "Bantam Books" and the portrayal of a rooster, is Registered in U.S. Patent and Trademark Office and in other countries. Marca Registrada. Bantam Books, Inc., 666 Fifth Avenue, New York, New York 10103.

PRINTED IN THE UNITED STATES OF AMERICA

H 0 9 8 7 6 5 4 3 2 1

For Chris

Thanks to Mike Antonucci for pointing the way. And special thanks to Elaine Markson, my agent; Alan Rinzler, my editor; and Barbara Alpert, his assistant, for making sure I got there.

I had never seen anyone hurt by a thing other than death or unbearable suffering except Hadley when she told me about the things being gone. She had cried and cried and could not tell me. . . . Then, finally, she told me. I was sure she could not have brought the carbons too and I . . . took the train for Paris. It was true all right and I remember what I did in the night after I let myself into the flat and found it was true.
—*A Moveable Feast*
by Ernest Hemingway

Whatever it was he did that December night remained his secret for the rest of his life.
—*Ernest Hemingway: A Life Story*
by Carlos Baker

FOREWORD

The mystery of Ernest Hemingway's lost manuscripts haunted me for nine years.

I first read about it in *A Moveable Feast*, read how in December, 1922, while covering an international peace conference in Switzerland, Hemingway, lonely and homesick, cabled his wife, Hadley, in Paris and asked her to join him in Lausanne.

Hadley agreed. And hoping to give her dashing young husband a surprise, she packed everything he had written up to the time—every short story and poem, even the genesis of a novel.

Her intentions were good. Lincoln Steffens, the famed muckraking journalist, also was at the peace conference. Steffens had taken an interest in Ernest's fiction and wanted to see more. This would be the perfect opportunity.

Or so Hadley thought.

But at Paris's Gare de Lyon, where she was to board a train bound for Lausanne, disaster struck. During a few minutes away from her luggage, the small valise with Ernest's manuscripts was stolen.

Hadley desperately searched the cavernous station but found no sign of the missing case.

Devastated, she arrived in Lausanne in tears, barely able to tell Hemingway that his life's work was gone.

Hemingway rushed back to Paris to see if the carbons to his precious manuscripts were still in the apartment on the rue du Cardinal Lemoine.

They were not.

In *A Moveable Feast*, Hemingway refers enigmatically to

what he did that night he discovered that the carbons too were lost.

The discovery must have been shattering. Try to imagine Hemingway as a young man, a struggling writer, laboring over each word, trying to make each story, each poem perfect.

As a fledgling writer myself, I shuddered to think how any writer could handle such a disaster. Certainly the fainter spirits would chuck the whole game, chalk it up to fate and pursue a saner career.

How had Hemingway felt? What had happened to his manuscripts? And what had he done on that mysterious night in Paris?

I had to find out.

I read every book, researched every possible source, confident that somewhere there was an answer to one of the great literary mysteries of the twentieth century.

There wasn't. I failed.

After college, I took a job as a copyboy with the *Daily News* in New York. I never forgot about Hemingway, never stopped wondering what anguish he must have felt when he realized that all his work was lost. I read every new book that came out about him and reread his novels and short stories.

But still there were no answers.

After several months as a copyboy, I was promoted to reporter. A year later, I was assigned to the one A.M. to nine A.M. shift, a dreadful tour reserved for young reporters like me and washed-up hacks like my partner, Seamus O'Reilly.

Incredibly, Seamus was the key that led to the solution to the mystery of the Hemingway manuscripts.

Seamus was an archetype—a grizzled veteran of forty-plus years on newspapers, a onetime star reporter who'd burned himself out years before by drinking too much late-night booze and cursing too many vindictive editors, brave deeds which won him a permanent slot on the graveyard trick.

Seamus ignored me for two weeks. Every night he went to sleep in a dark corner of the city room, leaving me responsible for the police and fire slips while juggling a slew of calls from the city's more communicative lunatics.

Imagine the weirdest characters from the strangest stories in the *National Enquirer* and you'll get some idea who calls a newspaper in the dead of night.

It got so bad that I wished O'Reilly would wake up and talk to me.

Three weeks into my tour of duty, my wish came true. O'Reilly, washed, shaved, neatly dressed and on the wagon, came in at precisely one A.M., looked at me across the city desk and said: "Who the hell are you?"

I told him. We chatted. By three, O'Reilly was regaling me with the colorful story of his life. Born in Paris in 1920, he was the son of the European correspondent for the old *Brooklyn Eagle*.

"Owen O'Reilly—my dad—was one hell of a great newspaperman. He knew everyone. FDR. Eisenhower. Patton. Benny Goodman. John D. Rockefeller. Hemingway. Lindbergh—"

"Hemingway?"

"Sure. My dad knew him in Paris before he hit it big. Great guy, Hemingway, but you didn't want to cross him even then. If provoked, he could be a dark and nasty bastard."

"Sometimes he didn't even need to be provoked."

O'Reilly unwrapped a meatloaf sandwich that oozed catsup. "What do you know about Hemingway?"

"Everything—with exceptions."

He offered me half his sandwich. I declined. "What do you mean 'with exceptions'?"

"I'll try not to sound too obsessive about this," I said. "In December, 1922, a suitcase containing everything Hemingway had written to that time was stolen from a train station in Paris. No one—including Hemingway—knows what happened to them. I've been trying to find out for years. I haven't had any luck."

O'Reilly ate his sandwich and sipped black coffee from a styrofoam cup. Broken blood vessels tattooed his bulbous nose. He wiped his mouth with a scrap of copy paper. I wondered how long he'd stay on the wagon.

"I think I can help you," he said.

"How?"

"Give me a minute to think." O'Reilly's bony hands covered his face. His gold cufflinks were emblazoned with his initials. "Damn it! I can see her clear as day."

"See who?"

"My father told me years ago," he said, ignoring my question. "What the hell was her name?"

The phone rang. "City desk," I said.

"A spaceship from Venus will land on Staten Island at precisely—"

I hung up. "So who is this mystery woman?"

O'Reilly shook his head. "Sorry, kid. I just can't remember."

I figured he'd been having too many one-sided conversations lately with Jack Daniels. "Don't worry about it."

"What time is it?"

I glanced at the four-faced clock above the city desk. "Almost four."

"It's okay then." O'Reilly picked up the phone and dialed.

"Who you calling?"

"My old man."

The idea that O'Reilly's father was still alive shocked me.

"Don't look so surprised, kid. The old man's only ninety-four. He lives in Flatbush."

"You sure you want to wake him up?"

"He doesn't sleep much. Most nights he's up watching the boob tube. It just takes him awhile to answer the phone."

Five minutes after dialing, O'Reilly said: "Dad? It's Seamus. How you doing?" He motioned for me to pick up the extension.

The elder O'Reilly's voice was surprisingly strong. "Are you drunk, Seamus?"

"No."

"Then you're a damn fool. What time is it?"

"Four."

"You shouldn't bother me now. Abbott and Costello are on television."

"This is important, Dad."

"Then spit it out, damn it."

"Sure, Dad. Do you remember a woman reporter who was a friend of Hemingway years ago?"

A minute of silence. I worried that the elder O'Reilly had died.

"Are you still with us, Dad?"

"Her name is Sara Morgan. I spent a wonderful night with her in Barcelona in 1926." He hung up. I wondered if the elder O'Reilly didn't sometimes call the city desk at night. He certainly sounded strange enough.

"There you have it," O'Reilly the younger said. "Sara Morgan."

I jotted down the name on a piece of copy paper, then

walked back to the library. There were dozens of clipping envelopes under Morgan but none for a Sara. *Who's Who* had nothing and less well-known reference books proved equally barren. I was about to return to the city room when the phone rang in the library.

It was O'Reilly. "The old man just called back. He remembered that Sara Morgan got married somewhere along the line to a guy named Hartunian. That shouldn't be hard to check out."

It wasn't. There was nothing in the clips, but *Who's Who* had a short entry, which I photostated. The only sign of Seamus when I returned to the city desk was a note stuck in my typewriter: "Kid, if you need me, I'm down in Louie's soothing a parched throat. S."

Louie's was a bar behind the *News* Building. Seamus had stepped off the wagon.

I didn't go to bed that morning when I got home. Instead, I brewed a pot of coffee and waited impatiently for noon. According to *Who's Who*, Sara Morgan was eighty-four years old and I didn't want to bother her until at least nine A.M. California time.

Two hours is a long time to brood about anything but I couldn't help myself. If all my Hemingway stuff wasn't buried under tons of debris in my closet, I'd have gone through it to reassure myself that my research deserved to be completed.

Thinking of Sara Morgan Hartunian, I reread the *Who's Who* entry:

HARTUNIAN, SARA MORGAN, writer: b. Rhinebeck, N.Y., July 26, 1897; s. Robert and Diana (Jenson) Morgan; ed. high sch., Rhinebeck; m. David Hartunian, 1935 (Dec. 1964), Reporter, Allied News Service, 1918–1927, N.Y. Graphic, 1927–1931. Author: *The Sutton Investigation*, 1931; *Hard and Soft*, 1932; *The Golden Mirror*, 1933, etc.; also (motion pictures) *Flaming Arrows; Sassy; Frontier Woman; Shanghai Clipper; Final Edition; Julia Claire*, etc. Home: P.O. Box 919 Carmel, Calif.

* * *

Would she talk to me? Did she know anything about Hemingway's lost manuscripts? Seamus O'Reilly claimed that she had been a close friend of Hemingway's in Paris, a confidante. "If anyone knows, she does," he had said. But Seamus was a lush. I had to talk to her myself.

Noon came. Taking a deep breath, I checked the photostat and called the Carmel operator for the number.

"I'm sorry, sir, but there is no listing under that name."

"Can you try just Morgan, operator. There must be a number."

"I'm sorry, sir. There's nothing."

I slammed the phone down and kicked the wall. Christ! There had to be some way to get in touch with her. I paced the living room, then stopped. What if she's dead? I thought. What if she'd died after *Who's Who* went to press? Damn . . .

I worked under the assumption that she was still alive. During the next two weeks, I exhausted every possibility. I telegrammed her. I wrote letters. I called people in Carmel—total strangers—and asked if they knew her.

Then I called the local newspaper.

"Carmel *Pine Cone*," said a friendly feminine voice.

"Hi. This is Vince Cosgrove. I'm a reporter from the *Daily News* in New York—"

"This is Chris Keller. I'm a reporter for the *Pine Cone*."

"That's a great name for a newspaper. Much better than *Daily News*."

She laughed politely. "Can I help you with something?"

"I hope so. I've been working on a story for a long, long time and I need to interview a woman named Sara Morgan Hartunian. I think she lives in Carmel."

"She sure does."

"You know her?"

"I house-sat for her a few years ago. She was going on a tour of the Canadian Rockies and she wanted someone to take care of her house."

"She must be active for her age."

"Extremely."

"Do you have any idea why she hasn't answered my letters? I've been trying to arrange an interview."

"She values her privacy. She doesn't even have a telephone anymore."

"Do you know if she's in Carmel now? She hasn't taken another vacation, has she?"

"No. I saw her yesterday fiddling around in her garden. She's here, all right."

"Thanks, Chris. If the *Daily News* can ever help the *Pine Cone*, let me know."

"I will. Goodbye."

I used the next weekend to fly to San Francisco. Once there, I rented a car and drove down the winding, breathtaking coast highway to Carmel.

Fog rolled in from the ocean as I swept past quaint gingerbread homes and even quainter shops. Carmel is the kind of place where the delicatessen is called a *charcuterie* and the Porsches seem to outnumber the people on the street.

Twice lost, I eventually found Sara's house, a small pink cottage atop a rocky precipice perched above a spectacular inlet. Seals and otters splashed in the waves below. I parked and walked along the cobbled path leading to the house. I stopped for a moment to watch the seals. The fog was so thick the Pacific seemed to disappear at the mouth of the inlet.

"Who are you?"

I whirled around.

A little old lady, gray-haired, prune-faced, and hunchbacked, was what I was expecting. Sara Morgan Hartunian—if this were she—was nothing like that geriatric cliché. This woman was slim and fashionably attired in designer jeans and a dark brown blouse. Her hair was white, her eyes blue and clear. Her face was not free of wrinkles but they seemed the wrinkles of someone middle-aged, not elderly. She was holding a dirt-caked hoe in her left hand.

"I'm looking for Mrs. Hartunian."

"Who are you?" she asked again.

I told her.

"You're the one from New York, aren't you? The one who's been sending me all those telegrams and letters."

"Guilty."

"You're certainly persistent."

"I'm a reporter. Persistence is a trick of the trade."

"A reporter, eh? Where do you work?"

"The *Daily News*."

"I was an old friend of Ed Sullivan," she said. "I remember when he started at the *News*. Did you know him?"

"Only from television."

The fog was thickening. I peered over my shoulder, now barely able to see any of the inlet. "Why didn't you answer my letters?"

"I like my privacy. It's why I got rid of the phone." She gave a slight smile. "And when you get to be my age, the temptation to live in the past is dangerously appealing. I have no particular affection for the concept of senility." Her throaty voice reminded me of Lauren Bacall's.

"I won't take much of your time."

She propped the hoe against the house. "I don't recommend your driving a car in this pea soup. And since my arthritis hates the damp, let's go inside. But don't ask me about Hemingway."

The house was larger than expected: a spacious, modern kitchen, two bedrooms, and a comfortable, booklined living room with a huge picture window of the fog-cloaked Pacific. A hearty fire burned in the fireplace.

"I'll get us some coffee," she said and went into the kitchen. I roamed the living room. One shelf was devoted to a series of hardcover and paperback mysteries which, judging from their covers, dated from the early 1930s to the late 1950s. They were all written by S. M. Jenson.

"I see you've spotted my collected works," Sara said as she carried in two steaming mugs of coffee.

"You're S. M. Jenson?"

"I was. But I retired him twenty-two years ago."

"Him?"

She laughed. "Those books are all hard-boiled thrillers. My publisher didn't want a woman's name on them so we came up with the pseudonym."

She sat on the couch. I settled into an overstuffed chair in front of the window.

"Great coffee," I said.

She reached across to an end table and opened a cigarette box. I moved to light her cigarette but she beat me to it. "I don't usually invite strangers in, you know."

"I'm flattered."

"You should be. If you weren't a reporter, I wouldn't have. But I'm a sucker for a newspaperman. Always have been."

"Is that because you were once one yourself?"

"Girl reporter was what they called us back then, back in the so-called good old days. Thank God some things have changed."

"What made you get out of newspapers?"

"Money. Unless you own them, there's no money—no real money—to be made in newspapers. I'd written a book and Jack Warner bought it and asked me to do the screenplay. So I quit. I was working at the New York *Graphic* at the time. There was a real rag, absolutely incredible. Then I came to California. Haven't left since."

"I didn't know you'd written movies." That was a lie. But I wanted her to loosen up and talk about her past.

"Dozens, most of them execrable. But they paid well. I like to say that this is the house that Jack Warner built."

"What happened?"

"Joe McCarthy happened. Don't ask me anymore. Suffice to say that my husband—who was a cameraman—and I became *persona non grata* in Hollywood. So we moved here."

The *Who's Who* entry had stated that her husband had died in 1964.

"My husband's real love was still-photography." She pointed to a dozen framed pictures above the mantle. All but one were nature shots in the Ansel Adams tradition. The exception was an eye-catching picture of a beautiful woman standing knee-deep in a stream. The woman was nude.

I whistled appreciatively.

"Don't be sexist."

"Sorry. But that's some picture."

"I was some subject."

"So I can see. In fact, you still look terrific."

She snuffed out her cigarette in a marble ashtray. "I attribute that to lots of smoking, lots of men, and not a lot of exercise," she said. "You're trying to charm me into telling you all about Hemingway."

"Another trick of the trade."

She leaned back in the couch. "No kidding. I suppose I should be angry, but hell, you did come three thousand miles—I guess I can indulge you a bit. But only a bit. What do you want to know?"

I wasn't sure where to start. "Well, a man named O'Reilly said that—"

"Owen O'Reilly? Is that son of a bitch still alive?"

"Sure is. He lives in Brooklyn."

"I'll be damned." She paused. I wondered if she was thinking of a night in Barcelona. "Give my regards to him if you see him."

"I will. But actually it was his son who said you'd been close to Hemingway in the 20s and that you might be able to help me out."

"With what?"

"For the past couple of years I've been trying to find out about a certain episode in Hemingway's life when a suitcase with all his work was stolen from the Gare de Lyon in Paris. I want to know what happened to those manuscripts and to Hemingway when he searched Paris for them."

Sara snapped on a lamp next to the couch, then abruptly turned it off. She stared at me for several moments. I'd obviously struck a nerve. "What's your interest in such ancient history?"

She listened attentively, shaking her head sympathetically as I described my frustrations and failures. By the time I was finished, it was dark outside and my throat ached from talking so much.

"So you think I have the answer," she said, lighting up another cigarette.

"You're the best lead I have."

Sighing, she stood and walked to the window. Despite her earlier reference to arthritis, there was no hint of age or affliction in her gait. I could easily see why Seamus O'Reilly had remembered her as a beautiful woman. She still was.

"I don't enjoy talking about Ernest," she said. "His memory is something I've always cherished. His death shocked me, depressed me. Even now, almost twenty years later, I can still shed a tear over him. He was the most talented American writer of this century. His contributions to literature were enormous. The people who criticize him, who belittle his achievements, those people aren't worthy enough to read his stories, let alone pretend to criticize them. He was a special person. A genius . . ."

Her back was to me and I couldn't be sure, but she seemed to be crying. A minute or so passed and she turned, her eyes clear, her voice steady. "He was one of the handsomest men I'd ever met. I used to joke that he belonged in a movie studio, not in some drafty garret on the Left Bank. When he walked into a room, people—especially women—watched him, went out of their way to talk to him, win his friendship, his love. Oh, I know all about his shortcomings—his temper, his pettiness, his vindictiveness. But those paled against his generosity and warmth and wisdom. He was a very special, very gifted man and I thank God I was lucky enough to know him."

Unsure what to say, I said nothing. Sara excused herself and disappeared into a back bedroom. Ten minutes later, I began to wonder if in some subtle way she had dismissed me. I walked around the living room, spying a shelf devoted to Hemingway, every book from *Three Stories and Ten Poems* to *Islands in the Stream*, all first editions. I pulled down *A Farewell to Arms*. I read the inscription: "To my trusted friend, Sara Morgan. Whose sense of loyalty was more important than her sense of journalism. Ernest."

What the hell did that mean? Hearing Sara padding down the hall, I slipped the book between *Men Without Women* and *Death in the Afternoon*, and returned to my seat.

"I'm sorry I took so long but I had a hell of a time finding this. It was in a closet buried under two moth-eaten mink stoles." Gently, she put a tattered brown box on the coffee table. "I hope the paper doesn't fall apart," she said, lifting out a three-inch thick ream of typewritten pages.

"What's that?"

"A book I wrote."

"About Hemingway?"

"That's right." She gazed fondly at the manuscript.

I could feel my nerves start their dog-fight routine. I knew—*I knew*—that the answer to the mystery that had haunted me for so long was in the manuscript.

"Do you know what Hemingway did that night in Paris? Is it in your book?"

"My dear young man, that *is* the book."

I was overwhelmed. There, two feet away, was the end to years of dead-ends, false starts, endless frustration and self-doubt. Somehow I controlled my instinct to grab the manuscript and run. "How come I never came across your book in my research?"

"Because I never published it."

"Why not?"

"I can't tell you very much. The book takes place in 1922. I wrote it six years later. It took only five weeks to write while I was in the south of France. I was always a fast writer. But don't get me wrong, a hell of a lot of research went into that book. I was still a newspaperman when I wrote it."

"So why didn't you publish if you'd done all that work?"

"By 1928, Ernest was a celebrity, a star. He'd amazed many people with *The Sun Also Rises*, and he was at work on a war novel—*A Farewell to Arms*—that everyone was waiting for expectantly. He was happily married to wife number two, Pauline. And people talked about him, people who usually didn't give a damn about books."

I wasn't completely following her, but I resisted interrupting.

"I'm telling you this so you'll know that I would have had no trouble finding a publisher. There was a market for a book about America's most prominent young man of letters, especially a book with many juicy parts. I wanted to write a best seller and the more I researched the story, the surer I became that I had a real page turner on my hands."

"You're doing a terrific job of whetting my appetite."

She laughed. "That's the mark of a good storyteller. Anyway, I finished the book and came back to America. Ernest and Pauline were in Florida. She was expecting a baby. I wrote him and he invited me down. I went. One night, after Pauline had retired, I showed Ernest the book."

"What happened?"

"He read it, every last word. I was never scared of Ernest but he could be an intimidating son of a bitch. Imagine sitting in the same room while Ernest Hemingway read your book! He didn't say anything for the three hours it took him to finish. I tried to get drunk but I was too nervous. Finally, he turned over the last page." Here, Sara did the same to the top page of her manuscript. "Then he stared at me. I fully expected to be the target of one of the famous Hemingway temper tantrums. Instead, the disarming bastard smiled and said I'd done a hell of a job."

"You're kidding?"

"Nope. He said: 'Kiddo, you've got yourself a real winner here. Should make you a bundle of dough.' There were a few mistakes, he said, but he still called it 'a first-rate job of reporting and writing.' Then he asked me not to publish it."

"Why?"

"For someone who didn't want to talk about Hemingway, I'm sure jabbering away."

"It's fascinating."

"I guess it is."

"So why didn't he want it published?"

She hesitated, then shrugged. "Publicity, primarily. He wanted to be considered a serious writer and he felt that my book would sabotage his efforts, bring him the kind of notoriety he didn't want. Even then he was concerned about his image."

"I hate to repeat myself, but why didn't he want it published?"

"You'd have to read my book to understand."

"Gladly."

"Now you're overestimating your powers of persuasion. Ernest asked me not to publish and I didn't. He also asked me to never—I repeat never—reveal to anyone what I had found out about his search for the missing manuscripts. I've honored that request for more than fifty years."

"I don't get it. You obviously put a great deal of time and effort into the book. Yet all Hemingway had to do was ask and you forgot the whole thing."

"I didn't forget. I just didn't publish."

"But why?"

"Am I smiling enigmatically?"

"I guess so—I've never been good at categorizing smiles."

"Well, you better get good because your only answer is going to be this silly grin."

I made one last try. "Can I read the book?"

"Of course not."

"I'm terrific at begging—I'll get down on my knees and grovel if it will help."

"I've always liked a reporter who'll do anything for a story, but the answer remains a firm and unequivocal no."

"But Hemingway's dead. What difference does it make?"

"I'm still alive, and still keeping my side of the bargain. And we're not going to discuss Hemingway anymore."

Clearly, she meant what she said. Defeated, I fell back in my chair and stared out the window. The fog had cleared away, revealing a cloudy, moon-lit horizon. "I better get going."

"Where are you staying?"

"No place yet—I didn't have the chance to find a room. Is that a problem?"

"Around here, one of the biggest. You're welcome to stay in the guest room."

I made some perfunctory protests but quickly accepted her invitation. Fatigue—brought on by jet lag and the sudden realization that I'd never solve the Hemingway mystery—consumed me. All I wanted was to sleep. But Sara had other plans.

"Do you like Japanese food?"

"I don't know. Never had it."

"I don't believe that."

"It's true. The idea of raw fish turns me off."

"For you I'll cook it." She went into the kitchen. "Just give me a few minutes—make yourself comfortable."

Kicking off my shoes, I stretched my legs along the coffee table. My toes brushed the yellowed pages of her manuscript. There was nothing to stop me from skimming the book. Sara couldn't see into the living room from the kitchen. It would have been easy to give a quick look.

I didn't touch the manuscript. Not then, and not after Sara's delicious dinner, when she insisted on doing the dishes alone. I stared a lot at the manuscript, sorely tempted to thumb through it, but I resisted.

After all, Sara had been kind and generous to me; reading her manuscript was no way to repay her. I had to honor her promise to Hemingway. I owed her.

She offered me a cordial. I declined and went to bed. A few minutes later, I heard her turn off the lights and retire to her bedroom. I wondered if the manuscript was still on the coffee table, begging to be read. Once, I'm ashamed to admit, I got halfway out of bed, then shook my head and slid back under the covers, falling asleep to the lulling sound of the waves breaking against the rocky inlet.

A discreet knock on the door awakened me at eight. "Breakfast in five minutes," said Sara. I took a quick shower and changed into a clean pair of pants and shirt.

Heading for the kitchen, I noticed that the manuscript was still on the coffee table. I kept moving.

Breakfast—an omelette, sausage, coffee, and homemade biscuits—was just as good as dinner. We ate on a deck overlooking the ocean. The fog had lifted completely and the antics of the seals and otters below made us laugh.

After breakfast, I persuaded Sara to let me do the dishes. Then I went into the guest room and packed my few belongings.

"You're welcome to stay as long as you like," Sara said.

"Thanks but this is Sunday. I have to be back in New York for work tomorrow."

"What are you talking about? This is only Wednesday."

"Maybe for you and the rest of the world, but I'm one of the lucky ones who has Tuesday and Wednesday off."

"God, I'd forgotten how miserable the newspaper business could be."

"Yeah." There was an awkward moment when neither one of us knew what to say or do. Then she walked over and hugged me, patting me on the back and saying, "Keep in touch. An old lady like me likes to hear from her friends."

"Old lady! You're one of the youngest people I know."

"And you're a terrible liar," she said, escorting me to the door.

"Thanks for everything," I said. "I'm glad I came."

"Even though you still don't know anything more about Hemingway?"

"Even though. Thanks again."

I was unlocking the car when she hurried out of the house, a brown package in her hand. My heart jumped. Was she giving me the manuscript?

"What's this?"

"A memento."

I started to open it. "No, no, no. You're not to do that until you're miles from here. I hate to give gifts—it embarrasses me." With that she disappeared into the house.

Mystified, I backed out of the driveway and headed north along the coast highway. I went exactly two miles before I stopped and ripped open the package.

It was her first edition copy of *A Farewell to Arms*, and under Hemingway's inscription she had written: "To someone who respects the meaning of trust. All the best, SMH."

For once, I actually felt good that I had ever gotten involved in the whole damn mess.

* * *

During the next year, Sara and I exchanged a half-dozen letters. Neither of us ever mentioned Hemingway. Then one day in December, her obituary appeared in *The New York Times*. It was just three paragraphs long, and traced her movie and book writing careers. She had had a heart attack at her home. She was eighty-five years old.

That night I said a silent prayer and offered a toast to her memory. I hoped that wherever she was she'd meet Hemingway and he'd buy her a drink. It was the least he could do.

I didn't give much thought after that to Hemingway, or, I'm sorry to confess, to Sara. By then I was off the dreaded lobster shift and working in the City Hall bureau, managing to keep busy.

Then, six weeks after her death, a package arrived via United Parcel. Inside was a letter and a cardboard box. The letter was from a lawyer in Carmel, informing me that I had been named in Sara's will and that my inheritance was enclosed.

Inside the box was Sara's Hemingway manuscript. She had added an introduction after my visit, explaining why, after so many years, she was allowing it to be published.

There was also a short note:

Dear Vince,

You'll probably be surprised to learn that I decided to give you the manuscript to my book the night you visited me in Carmel. I couldn't then—you'll understand why when you read the introduction.

I was testing you, you know, by leaving you alone with the manuscript. I value honor. I wanted to see if you did, too.

The manuscript is yours. God knows that by the time you read this, I'll have no use for it. So do with it what you will—publish it, shred it, make it into an air force of paper airplanes.

It's up to you.

SMH

I've read the manuscript more than a dozen times, always fascinated by Sara's tale.

Do I believe it?

Well, the reader should remember that Sara was a novelist

and screenwriter—occupations which rely on a fertile imagination. And even she admits in her introduction to taking certain liberties. What those liberties are, I do not know.

I do know that I want to believe the book.

Why?

Because if it didn't happen the way Sara says, it's a hell of a shame.

Vincent Cosgrove
New York City, 1983

INTRODUCTION

I first met Ernest Hemingway at the Brasserie Lipp on the Boulevard Saint-Germain on July 26, 1922. I remember the date because it was my twenty-fifth birthday and I was feeling suitably sorry for myself—a man I thought I'd been in love with had broken our engagement just a week before. Even though I decided that I never really loved him, depression still set in and even Paris turned bleak, if only for a while.

I was just finishing my third Scotch and soda when Hemingway came into Lipp's at about ten P.M. He wore a tweed jacket and tan slacks and his flannel shirt was open at the neck. As he walked past my table, I figured he was too damn attractive to be anything but an actor.

For the next several minutes, I pretended not to notice him as he leaned against the bar, drinking beer and studying what appeared to be a racing form. While not in the habit of approaching strangers, the Scotch fortified me enough to abandon my table—and inhibitions—and squeeze in next to him at the bar.

"*Parlez-vous Anglais?*" I asked in my less-than-perfect French.

He looked up from the tout sheet. "I hope so or the folks back in Illinois would be ashamed of me." His soft, gentle voice belied his dark, rather cruel good looks.

Like a schoolgirl, I groped for something—anything—to say. "I was hoping you were an American."

"Really? Why?"

"You know—stranded in a foreign city, surrounded by strangers, all that business."

"What you mean is you're lonely."

"Exactly."

"How long have you been here?"

"Two months."

"Let's have a drink." He ordered a beer for himself and another Scotch for me.

"How did you know I was drinking Scotch?" I asked a bit more coquettishly than I care to remember.

"I saw you when I came in. It is Scotch, isn't it?"

"Yes." I was flattered he'd noticed.

"What's your name?"

"Sara Morgan."

"Ernest Hemingway." We shook hands.

Over drinks, we synopsized our lives: I was a correspondent for the Allied News Service; he was a reporter who'd been in the war, returned home, then escaped to Paris to write fiction—a pursuit so unsuccessful that he still freelanced for the *Toronto Star*.

The fact that we both had toiled in the Fourth Estate was reason enough for another round of drinks. And another and another. Time passed quickly; Ernest was an excellent storyteller, and he beguiled me with tales of the war, Kansas City, and his hometown near Chicago.

By midnight, I knew I'd found a friend and wondered if I'd also found a lover. Then he looked at my watch and said he had to go home because his wife would be worried.

"Your wife?"

"Sure. Didn't I tell you I was married?"

"I guess it slipped your mind."

Paying the bill, he offered to take me home.

"I wouldn't want you to get in trouble with your wife."

"I said she'd be worried, not angry. Don't worry about me," he said.

A cab was waiting at the curb. I said nothing as we sat in the back seat. I debated with myself whether I really had any right to be mad at him. Had he been leading me on? Had he deliberately not mentioned his wife? As the taxi turned onto the rue Maître-Albert—my street—I decided to give him the benefit of the doubt.

"Would you like to come up?"

"I'd like nothing more but I'm married, remember?"

"It makes no difference to me." I felt somewhat ridiculous saying that, but at that particular moment it really did make no difference.

"But it does with me," he said. He kissed me chastely on the cheek. "Come around some night and let's have dinner."

"You, me, and your wife?"

"Sure—she's a wonderful girl. You'll love her."

I never put myself through that particular torture, but Ernest and I met regularly, sometimes for lunch, usually for an early evening drink. He talked passionately about writers and writing. I was a captive audience.

At first he brought clippings of his newspaper stuff. Later, he let me read some of his fiction. His work was superb, better than anything I'd ever seen from a so-called inexperienced writer.

Our relationship never went beyond friendship. Despite my most assiduous attempts, we never had an affair. I hope he had his regrets. I certainly did.

The last time I saw Ernest was in Florida in 1928. I had written this book and I wanted his reaction. While he praised my effort, he asked me not to publish. I agreed.

Why, then, am I publishing the book now?

My agreement with Ernest was not to publish in "our lifetime." While Ernest died in 1961, I had the fate to live to a ripe old age.

Once I'm gone, however, there is no reason not to finally publish. For one thing, I worked too hard on the damn book for it to languish in some dusty closet. And far too many years have passed for any revelation within these pages to do any harm to Ernest's reputation.

Besides, Ernest's fears, I always thought, were unfounded. As you'll see, he comes across quite well in the book.

Since, quite clearly, I will not be around to answer personally, I must now anticipate the reader's questions. Some may wonder how I can describe so many scenes when I was not a witness to ninety-nine percent of the narrative. How do I know what happened to Ernest at Harry's Bar? How do I know what he said to James Joyce at the Deux Magots? How do I know what he—and others—were thinking?

The answer is simple: good, old-fashioned legwork. I devoted a great deal of time to the project, researching events, interviewing scores of people, tracking down obscure sources to fill the tiniest gap in the story.

I admit to applying the technique of the novel to nonfiction (and I wish Truman Capote and Norman Mailer would stop taking bows for this). Not every scene is an exact reflection of reality. But I hope that the book's spirit comes as close as possible to the truth.

One final warning: a character named Sara Morgan appears in several scenes. While I have no great affection for writing about myself in the third person (unlike some of our more celebrated "new journalists"), I concluded that confusion would be the only offspring of any other possible approach.

I beg the reader's indulgence.

Sara Morgan Hartunian
Carmel-by-the-Sea
November 12, 1982

CHAPTER 1

The mandarin had frozen solid.

Ernest Hemingway palmed the orange in his left hand and squeezed. It was as hard and appetizing as a golf ball. Just might thaw by spring, he thought. Angrily, he threw the fruit across the room and into the fireplace, where it sizzled in the embers and popped. Rest in peace.

The room was on the top floor of a crumbling hotel on the rue Descartes. It was the hotel where the poet Paul Verlaine had died years before. Ernest liked the room. It was cheap and quiet and a good place to work. Sometimes late at night, if the writing was difficult and he was tired, he liked to stretch out on the straw-filled mattress and rest his eyes. He liked to imagine Verlaine's ghost gliding gently through the hotel, haunting the rooms, a disembodied voice whispering: *"Pourquoi triste, o mon âme— Triste jusqu'à la mort...."*

There was no ghost tonight and no need for Ernest to rest. The writing had gone well. He had started and finished a short story in one sitting. It was about a young man just returned from the war who goes on a fishing trip with his father. The young man soon resents the old man's failure to understand how the war has changed him. They quarrel and the young man leaves his father, finds a canoe and paddles up river, swearing to himself that he will never return. But even as he paddles, the young man knows that he will go back. There is no place else to go.

Ernest flipped through the blue-covered notebook in which he had written the story. Sometimes he wrote in longhand, constantly sharpening his pencil until it was too short to hold and he'd have to take out another. Other times, he used the battered but dependable Corona typewriter Hadley, his wife, gave him last year for his twenty-second birthday.

Tonight he had written in pencil and the words came as quickly as he could get them down. It wasn't always like that, wasn't always that easy. Which was why he was so angry that the mandarin had frozen.

He planned the mandarin to be his reward. Always before starting to write, he promised himself a reward: write well and you can have a bottle of wine, or that book you've been waiting to buy at Sylvia Beach's. Sometimes it was just a piece of fruit, depending on finances. If the writing was bad, there was no reward.

Tonight he deserved a reward. The story was a good one and he wanted in some small way to celebrate. But he'd stupidly left the mandarin on the windowsill. Damn.

He got up from behind the small desk and stretched, raising his arms until his fingertips brushed the low ceiling. He stood six feet tall and was solidly built. His face was dark and he'd recently grown a mustache, hoping to add a touch of maturity to his youthful good looks. On first meeting, many people took him for a professional athlete—a misconception he never tried to correct.

Walking to the window, he looked out on the shadowy eaves and gables of the Latin Quarter. The only light—pale and silvery—came from the nearly full moon. On the roof below, a black cat skulked. Superstitiously, Ernest turned away before the cat crossed his line of vision. He slipped his right hand into his pocket and touched the worn rabbit's foot he always carried.

He decided to reward himself with a drink at the Amateurs. It wasn't much of a reward but it was a hell of a lot better than a rock-hard mandarin.

Before putting his coat on, he remembered to date the story. Opening the notebook to the last page, he wrote: November 22, 1922.

Ernest almost stumbled in the pitch-black landing outside his room. His right leg buckled and he braced his hands against the wall. His legs were full of shrapnel, dozens of tiny souvenirs from a night in Italy when he had played hero and carried a wounded soldier to safety. The guy was hurt by the same Austrian shell that had sliced up Ernest's legs. Somehow, Ernest got him back to the command post, but not before an

Austrian machine gunner added insult to injury and sprayed several bullets into Ernest's already damaged legs.

But it had been worth it. Italy gave him one of its highest honors, the *Croce di Guerra*. And he had a hell of a story to tell people back home. The legs rarely bothered him.

Downstairs, in the peeling, urine-reeking hole that passed for the hotel's lobby, the blubbery night clerk sat behind the registration desk, munching an apple tart and reading a pornographic novel.

"You'll have to go to confession tomorrow," Ernest said.

The clerk gave him the finger. Ernest wondered if the clerks did that at the George V.

He pulled his collar up and dug his hands into his coat pockets. The streets were empty. Even a night city like Paris couldn't muster much action on a freezing cold Wednesday evening. He hurried around the corner to the Café des Amateurs.

The Amateurs was a human sewer, a dark and dirty cafe with a dance floor covered with sawdust and a wooden bar scarred with the initials of drunken customers. The place attracted a mixed crowd: soldiers, sailors, whores, petty thieves, neighborhood characters, even an occasional literary fugitive from Montparnasse. Entering the Amateurs, Ernest hoped that the literary types had stayed home.

Two sailors and a pasty-faced whore stood at the bar, negotiating a fair price for services soon to be rendered. Jerome, the emaciated bartender with a tubercular cough, leaned against the bar and smiled knowingly. Jerome always smiled knowingly, leading Ernest to conclude that Jerome knew nothing at all.

Two men and a woman sat at the table in the back. Ernest knew one of the men, a no-talent hack named Leo Nelson. Ernest didn't want to talk to Nelson, who was a bore. The ease with which Ernest had written the short story had left him feeling good and he didn't want Leo Nelson to change that.

Keeping his back to Nelson's table, he ordered a Scotch.

"Monsieur is working late tonight," Jerome said.

"Monsieur *was* working late—now he's on holiday."

"Monsieur should find someplace nicer for a holiday," Jerome said. Jerome hated working in the Amateurs. His goal was to tend bar at the Ritz. He had a long way to go.

"This place fulfills my need to observe humanity at its worst," Ernest said. Jerome flashed one of his patented smiles. "You know, Jerome, if you ever do get to work at the Ritz that smile will make you a rich man. All a drinking customer wants is a bartender who always agrees with him and smiles."

"Monsieur is too kind."

Ernest threw the whiskey down. It was tasteless and burned his throat. France was a hell of a lot closer to Scotland than America, but Paris bars served lousy Scotch. He didn't know why. Harry's served good Scotch, but it was too cold and too late to go to Harry's. Ernest ordered another Scotch.

"Hemingway! Is that you?"

Ernest reluctantly turned around. "Hello, Nelson. I didn't see you in the shadows."

Nelson was in his forties, paunchy and short. He sweated a great deal and his few remaining wisps of blond hair always seemed pasted to his scalp. He was English and pretentious, given to such non sequiturs as, "When I was at Oxford," or "H. G. Wells said to me only the other day . . ." Ernest thought that Nelson was a consummate ass.

Nelson introduced Ernest to his companions. The woman had a face covered with too much makeup and black hair cut severely short. "This is Jacqueline," Nelson said. "She sculpts."

Jacqueline gave Ernest an appraisal, then nodded approval. "A pleasure," she said. Ernest wondered if she was any good in bed.

"And I'm sure," Nelson said, "that you know Clive Russet."

"Only by reputation," said Ernest, shaking Russet's hand. Russet was a literary legend—publisher, editor, essayist. He was known in England for his patronage of struggling writers and his friendship with established ones, many of whom he had helped to discover. He had a long, rather sad face, pale blue eyes and a pencil-thin moustache.

Ernest would never consider having a drink with Nelson. But Russet was an influential man, someone who could make a writer's career. Ernest sat.

"You're American, aren't you?" Russet said.

"Born and raised in Illinois."

"My friend James Joyce has told me about you. He thinks you're very talented."

"He's a generous man."

Nelson, who had had to pay a vanity press to print his own novel, cut in. "We were just talking about *The Rotted Barrel*."

"I'm afraid I haven't read it."

Nelson chuckled. "Of course not, dear boy. It's a play."

Embarrassed, Ernest wanted to hit Nelson.

"If Leo hadn't dragged me to see it, I wouldn't have known what it was either," Russet said diplomatically. "Leo thinks it's a work of art and I think it's a—"

"Piece of shit!" Jacqueline exclaimed. Something lightly touched Ernest's right leg and moved slowly up and down. Jacqueline stared at Ernest, smiling slightly. Ernest didn't find her attractive enough to return the caress.

"I wouldn't go quite that far—I'd call it an interesting but failed experiment," said Russet. "Are you writing anything I'd be interested in, Mr. Hemingway?"

Before Ernest could answer, Nelson spoke. "Really, Clive, I have to disagree. Clairoux, the playwright, was trying something new and different. He was . . ."

Ernest could tell that Nelson's lecture bored Russet. The sculptress stopped playing footsies and settled back in her chair, waiting for Ernest to make a move. He did nothing to encourage her.

Instead, he watched and listened as Nelson droned on about the play. Russet occasionally interjected an opinion but mostly it was Nelson's show.

Ernest tried to remember what they were saying, how they looked, what little gestures they used as they spoke. This was a habit of his, and he did it because it was what a writer should do: listen and observe and get it down on paper if it was worth writing about.

Sometimes he forgot, but usually his memory was good, so that later, if he were writing, he'd get it down, not necessarily verbatim; people's exact conversations were rarely memorable. What he would write would be close to reality but filtered through his own perception and imagination. In his more serious moments, usually when the day's mail included a rejection slip, he reassured himself that this was his talent, his gift.

Nelson was now talking about Gertrude Stein, who apparently had turned thumbs down on the play.

"Of course, Gertrude hated it but that's understandable because the play's about sex," Nelson said.

"What do you mean?" asked Russet. Ernest sensed that Russet was losing patience with Nelson.

"Gertrude Stein couldn't possibly appreciate a work of art in which sex—normal sex—is the theme."

Ernest liked Gertrude Stein very much. She praised his work and gave him some helpful suggestions. He was less fond of Alice B. Toklas, Stein's companion, but he still objected to Nelson's snide innuendo.

"What are you talking about, Nelson?" Ernest asked.

"Don't be so naive. She's a follower of Sappho, my dear boy. A lesbian. You do know what that means, don't you?"

Ernest figured he had two choices: he could get up and leave, or he could clock Nelson a good one to the head. Nelson wasn't much of a match, Ernest admitted. But he sensed that Russet was as offended by Nelson's remarks as he was. And Ernest wanted to impress Russet.

"Miss Stein is a friend of mine," Ernest said. "I don't think I like what you're saying."

"Face it—a dyke is a dyke is a dyke, as Gertrude might say."

That wasn't a bad line coming from a faker like Nelson. Under other circumstances, Ernest would have laughed. But he wanted to score points with Russet and laughter wasn't the way to do that.

Ernest worked fast, standing and reaching across the table, grabbing Nelson by the collar and swinging him around so they were face to face. A glass of beer overturned and shattered on the floor. Ernest pushed Nelson away, hesitated for a moment to decide where he should hit him, then snapped his right fist out, brushing against Nelson's jaw. It was a half-baked punch, a woman's punch, but it was enough to send Nelson to the floor.

The sculptress produced a little yelp and ran to Nelson's side. A thin line of blood trickled from the corner of his mouth.

"You're a bully," she said, looking up at Ernest. "A bully!"

Ernest laughed. He hadn't been called a bully since he was fifteen. His mother had called him that after he'd beat up two smaller friends in a makeshift boxing ring they'd set up in her music room. *Bully*. It hadn't bothered him then and it didn't bother him now.

"I'll get you for this, Hemingway," Nelson said.

"Oh Lord, I'm shaking with fear," Ernest said mockingly. "Please, Leo, take it back. Tell me you'll forgive me. If you don't I won't be able to sleep."

"Go to hell," Nelson said. Supported by the sculptress, he started out of the cafe.

Russet remained seated, stroking his chin with his fingers. The look of indifference confused and worried Ernest. Had he made a mistake by lashing out at Nelson?

But as soon as Nelson was gone, Russet burst into laughter. "That was wonderful—I can't tell you how many times I wanted to do that."

"Is he a friend of yours?" asked Ernest, enormously relieved that his gamble had paid off.

"Christ, no. He's my wife's cousin. I put up with him only out of familial loyalty."

"I really couldn't let him get away with what he said about Miss Stein," Ernest said, trying to sound morally indignant. "Even if it's true."

"Of course not—some things are better left unsaid." Russet pushed his chair back and stood. "I'm afraid that I have to be going. Unfortunately, I'm staying with Leo and it won't look right if I don't go back with him."

"I was hoping we could talk."

"What about dinner tomorrow night? I'll get Joyce to come."

"That sounds fine," Ernest said, then remembered something. "Damn, I'm leaving for Switzerland tomorrow. I have to cover the peace conference in Lausanne for the wire services."

Russet screwed up his face in disgust. "Get out of daily journalism as fast as you can. It's ruined more writers than liquor, women, and angst combined."

"I'm going to quit as soon as I can afford to."

"Make it soon. If you're ever in London, look me up. And send me one of those stories Joyce was so high on."

Russet shook Ernest's hand and left. Ernest turned to finish his drink. Seconds later, the sculptress reappeared.

"Are you going to shoot me?" asked Ernest as she opened her beaded purse.

"Pistols are phallic symbols—I suspect they're your department." She took out a pen and a piece of paper and began to write. "Here's my address and telephone number." She handed the note to him.

"I thought I was a bully."

"An interesting trait. Come to my studio. I like to sculpt men in the nude. I'd like to sculpt you."

He laughed. "Who's in the nude? You or your subject."

"Both—if things get interesting." Ernest watched her leave. Her hips swayed provocatively as she walked. Her ass looked firm, if a little too large. She wasn't the first woman in Paris who'd come on to him. Pocketing the slip of paper, he wondered when he'd take one up on it.

Hadley Hemingway was reading in bed when Ernest came in. It was cold in the apartment and she was snuggled under several layers of blankets and quilts.

"I thought you'd be asleep," he said, hanging his coat in the armoire.

"It's too cold to sleep." She rested the book on the night table. It was Conrad's *Lord Jim*. Ernest had urged her to read it.

Hadley didn't look eight years older than Ernest. But she was. She had a youthful face framed by rich auburn hair cut fashionably short. (But not, Ernest thought happily, as short as the pushy sculptress in the Amateurs.)

Hadley bristled whenever Ernest teasingly told her that she looked "sweet and innocent." She blamed her full face and what she called her "squirrel's cheeks" for making her appear that way. She was too old to be either sweet or innocent, she complained. Besides, she'd spent too long being that way, at least before she'd met Ernest.

"You should have started a fire," Ernest said and began to undress.

"We're short of coals."

He slipped out of his pants. "I'll get some before I leave tomorrow." He put on his nightshirt and sat next to Hadley on the bed.

"You deserve better than this," he said, stroking her hair. They were living off Hadley's small trust fund and whatever he earned from his journalism. It was enough to feed them but not enough to get them out of the cramped, two-room apartment on the fourth floor of the building at 74, rue du Cardinal Lemoine.

"You don't hear me complain, do you? I'm happy. I love Paris and I love you." She laced her hands around his neck and pulled him down, kissing him passionately. Hadley looked like the girl next door, which was why the intensity of her lovemaking always surprised Ernest.

She broke the kiss. "Did you finish the story?"

"Sure did."

"I want to read it."

"Wait till the morning."

"No. I want to read it now."

Ernest sighed and reluctantly pulled away. "You're getting to be a real pain in the ass," he said and grinned.

She propped herself up with two pillows, then kissed him again on the mouth. "Just get the story and shut up."

Obediently, he dug the notebook out of his coat and gave it to her. While she read, he spread the remains of old newspapers in the fireplace and struck a match, watching the flames devour the paper. The fire was nearly out by the time Hadley finished the story.

"It's very good, Ernest. One of your best."

"But?"

"But what?"

"I can tell from the tone of your voice that you have reservations."

"Well—"

"Come on, Hadley. What is it? What's wrong?" He fought a rush of anger. Taking criticism from Gertrude Stein was all right; he wasn't sure about taking it from Hadley. She was very bright, but literary criticism was not her strongest point.

"It's just that I don't think the father should be so cold to his son."

Ernest knew why. Hadley had fond memories of her own father. He had been kind and loving and generous with all his children. His suicide, when she was eight, had been the worst shock of her life.

"Fathers can be unbearably cool to their sons. And vice versa." He thought of his own father, a distant man.

"But this father is such an extreme."

Ernest smiled. Two years ago, Hadley never would have criticized his work. She was too shy, too reserved. But lately she had become more assertive, more self-confident. Part of it, he felt, was the liberating effect of Paris. And part of it—the largest part—was his influence on her.

He took the story from her. "The father has to be extreme. If he weren't, there'd be no story. Who wants to read about two people who get along all the time?"

"Does that mean you'll never write about us?"

"The Hemingways of Paris, France? We're too boring."

"Why don't you come back to bed and do something about our boring plight."

"Don't go away." He went into the living room and dropped the notebook in the bottom drawer of his desk. The drawer was stuffed with short stories, poems, and even the beginning of a novel, everything he had worked on since they'd arrived in Paris.

Hadley had turned off the bedroom light and taken off her nightgown. Ernest got into bed. They moved against each other, their hands touching, exploring.

After they made love, Ernest lay awake, watching shafts of moonlight stretch across the ceiling. He felt pleased with himself. He had written a good story. He had met and impressed Clive Russet. Hadley loved him.

He had no complaints.

CHAPTER 2

At about the same time that Ernest was dropping off to sleep, a tall, thin man wearing a full-length leather coat worn rough in several spots moved deeper in a shadowy doorway across the street from the Gilbert Asylum in Montmartre. After four hours there, the cold was beginning to take its toll. He clapped his gloved hands and stomped his freezing, aching feet.

Three- and four-story apartment buildings dominated the street, a typical working-class neighborhood, no artsy types here. The architectural exception was the asylum, a red-brick manse set back from the curb and protected by an eight-foot-high iron fence ribboned with ivy. A single light—the only one in the street—gleamed from a first-floor room near the front door.

A figure appeared at the corner. The man in the doorway stepped back further. The figure crossed the street, coming straight for the darkened doorway. The man's hand reached into his coat pocket and tightened around the handle of the Colt .45 automatic, made in America, bought on the black market.

The figure stopped directly in front of the doorway. A man, short, head cocked to the right and slightly forward, peered in. "Herr Goering?" the man said. "Are you there, Herr Goering?"

The man in the doorway released his grip on the gun. Hermann Goering was a cautious man who believed in taking no unnecessary risks. This was not a risk. He slowly inched out of the shadows to let Kurdorf—stupid, insipid Kurdorf—see him.

"I told you," Goering said carefully, "to stay in the car."

Kurdorf stepped into the doorway, his myopic eyes squinting behind his glasses. "We were wondering how much longer we were going to have to stay tonight."

"Until he comes."

"This is the third night. Perhaps he'll never appear."

"Then prepare yourself for a long stay in Paris."

An asthmatic wheeze hissed from Kurdorf's parted lips. "The cold is no good for me."

"Munich is also cold," said Goering, trying to modulate his voice and not show his anger toward Kurdorf. It was difficult. Goering had little respect for a man who failed to follow orders. Besides, Kurdorf was only an informant, a spy ordered by their superiors to make sure everything was reported to Munich.

"Why don't you go back to the car?" Goering suggested.

"Those two musclemen bore me. All they talk about is soccer and beer. I have no interest in either." Kurdorf sniffled and wiped his nose. "And I was hoping you could tell me more about our mission."

"What do you want to know? You already know that we're waiting for a man named Burchardt to arrive and take a woman out of the asylum—a woman named Anna Aronson. That's not her real name. We've been ordered to kidnap her. What more is there?"

"Well, the woman is supposed to be a Russian duchess, right? What's a duchess doing in an asylum?"

Goering spoke slowly, not wanting to confuse Kurdorf. "She came to Paris several months ago. No one, including the White Russians here, would have anything to do with her. To them she was an impostor, one of a hundred fakes. She never got past their servants. When no one acknowledged her, she tried to kill herself by jumping into the Seine. She was rescued and brought to the asylum."

"So what makes her different from all other impostors?"

"She is said to possess certain documents—special documents—which conclusively prove her claim. And for the last three years, the White Russian community has speculated, many have believed, that the real duchess has been living on Burchardt's estate near Werneuchen."

"Outside Berlin? I hear it's beautiful there."

"It is. Anna Aronson has lived there as a recluse. For

reasons unknown, she left and came to Paris. Burchardt, our sources say, has convinced her to return with him."

"So Burchardt's coming to this asylum, plus the documents, make her the real duchess."

"We think so. And so do others."

"Then these documents are important."

"They are vital, particularly to us. We can make a fortune with them. But without them, she is completely worthless, another impostor, even with Burchardt by her side."

"And we're sure she has them with her?"

"That's what we've been told. With luck, we'll find out tonight." There was more Kurdorf could know, but Goering thought he had conveyed enough information for one session. He took out a flask, uncapped it, swallowed some brandy, then offered the flask to Kurdorf.

Kurdorf took several sips, warmed almost as much by Goering's apparent confidence in him as by the liquor. He was a very lucky man, he thought, to be working with such a great war hero as Hermann Goering.

"Something wrong, Kurdorf?"

"Nothing. Why do you ask?"

"You were staring at me."

"Was I? I'm sorry. I must be tired."

"Go back to the car."

"I'll stay here if you don't mind. I'd rather be cold than sit in the car and listen to these two bores."

"Suit yourself."

They stood silently in the doorway and waited. They both wondered about the woman in the asylum, wondered if her claims were true, wondered if she really was the Grand Duchess Anastasia, the last surviving child of the Czar of Russia.

Fifteen blocks away, a gleaming Rolls-Royce Twenty coasted along the Boulevard Rochehouart.

Sitting in the back seat, the rich leather crinkling under his weight, Nicholas Burchardt opened the fully stocked bar under the right window. He took the top off a jeweled samovar and poured a cup of tea, adding a generous splash of vodka.

Sipping the tea, he rubbed his hand against the side of the window and cleared away the frost. He had been to Paris enough times in the last few months to know that they'd be at the asylum in a few minutes.

Burchardt was pleased. The streets were deserted, save for an occasional baker's truck on its way to a *boulangerie*. He had been troubled by rumors that a group of White Russians was planning a kidnapping. Others, probably Bolsheviks, were also said to be interested.

The French government had refused to supply protection for the woman in the asylum, scoffing at the idea that she was Anastasia. Burchardt didn't blame the French—her claim *was* unbelievable.

So without official protection, Burchardt had decided to pick her up in the middle of the night, hoping to catch any would-be kidnappers off guard. The people in the asylum knew only that he would arrive within the week with the necessary papers needed to release the woman. They did not know exactly when. No one did. Even his family—his wife, son, and daughter—knew nothing of his plans. A cautious man, he believed in taking as few risks as possible.

"How's the driving?"

Curt Zyklon, his chauffeur, said over his shoulder: "Beautiful. The streets are icy but you'd never know it from the way she handles." Curt, who had driven the car from Berlin, had been with him for years. He was a big, lumbering man who spoke only when spoken to. He never gossiped, a valuable asset in an employee. Before they had checked out of their hotel, Burchardt had given Curt a pistol. Merely a precaution. You could never be too safe.

The Rolls turned onto the Boulevard Barbès. High on a hill to the left, outlined in the moonlight, stood the Sacré-Coeur Basilica, its great dome and cupolas reminding Burchardt of churches in his native Russia. He hadn't been back to Russia in thirty years. Yet hardly a day went by when he didn't think of his parents and friends, nothing but memories.

Germany had been good to him: a job in a steel mill, promotions, a fortuitous marriage to the owner's daughter. Now he owned the plant. In Russia, he'd still be a peasant. But in Germany he was a man of affluence, a man who commanded respect.

Despite it all, he still thought of himself as a Russian. And he always would. It was why he had befriended Anastasia and taken her into his home. As a Jew, he had no love for the Romanovs. Czarist rule through the years was marked by cruelty and stupidity. But Anastasia was a young woman who had lived through a particularly gruesome kind of hell, a woman who needed a great deal of love and protection. In the simplest terms, she was a Russian who needed help.

He thought of the woman in the asylum. Confused, frightened, suspicious. It had made no sense for her to run away to Paris. Her home was with him and his family. He had spent months convincing her to return with him. He knew it would be for the better.

Eventually, so would she.

Goering pulled out his pocket watch. Three-fifteen. Even he was beginning to have doubts about Burchardt's arrival, was resigned to having wasted yet another night. He was about to tell Kurdorf they'd quit until tomorrow night when a limousine idled down the street, rolling gently to a stop in front of the asylum.

"Is that Burchardt?"

"I doubt anyone else would show up here in a Rolls-Royce."

They watched a heavyset man dressed in a dark overcoat, a gray homburg perched on his head, get out of the Rolls, walk to the front gate and push a button. A bell from the asylum dimly echoed across the street. A white-frocked orderly opened the asylum door and came down the steps to the gate.

The man from the Rolls displayed some papers. Words were exchanged. The orderly unlocked the gate and the two men went inside.

"That's Burchardt," said Goering. "Go back to the car and tell them to get ready." Goering quickly placed a restraining hand on Kurdorf's arm. "Burchardt's chauffeur is still in the car. Don't let him see you."

Kurdorf gave a little salute and moved down the street, dodging in and out of the shadows. The chauffeur didn't notice him.

Goering took out his .45, released the safety. His hand

shook a bit, not from nervousness, but anticipation. It had been four years since he'd seen any real action.

Too long.

A young doctor, fresh from sleep, eyes blinking in the light, hands busily tucking his shirttails into his pants, approached Burchardt in the drab lobby of the asylum.

"Yes? What is it?"

Burchardt showed him the release papers. The doctor told the orderly to fetch the patient in room 514.

"It's a rather strange time for this sort of thing," the doctor said.

Burchardt crossed his arms, said nothing.

"She doesn't talk a great deal. Keeps to herself," said the doctor.

"She's always been that way," Burchardt said.

"When she first came here she wouldn't speak at all. We finally won her confidence, at least a little. That was when she made her grand announcement."

"Do you believe her?"

"That she's the daughter of the Czar? Don't make me laugh. But I do believe that she thinks she is. She certainly acts like royalty."

Burchardt hadn't noticed that during his previous visits. "What do you mean?"

The doctor rubbed his bloodshot eyes. "When she does talk, it's usually a command. 'Do this. Do that.' You'll find out."

The orderly came into the lobby, a suitcase in each hand. Behind him stood a woman, about twenty years old, with black hair and a face that at one time may have been pretty but was no longer. She had dark eyes, a broad nose, and prominent chin. Her jaw looked slightly out of line, as if it had been broken and improperly set. Several short, thin scars lined her neck. Her simple brown dress was faded, its hem tattered. Her dirty cloth coat was bulky, a size too large.

The orderly put the suitcases down and disappeared down the hall. No one spoke.

Standing there, Burchardt felt strangely intimidated. She stared at him, he felt, as if she were expecting him to bow.

He didn't move.

She slowly raised her right arm, pointing with her index finger to the suitcases. She wanted him to carry them. Without a word, she brushed past him and walked out of the asylum.

"At least she opened the door for herself," the doctor said sympathetically.

Burchardt picked up the suitcases, which were light. "Thank you, doctor."

She was standing imperiously near the car, her head thrown back in some strange, dramatic pose. As Burchardt placed the suitcases in the trunk, he wondered if she weren't better off in the asylum.

In the car, Burchardt tapped the glass partition and signaled Curt to start off. There was only the slightest jolt as the Rolls came to life and moved quietly down the street.

"Well?" she said in Russian. Once again, she pointed with her right hand, this time to the open bar next to Burchardt.

"What is it?"

"Tea, of course. I haven't had an acceptable cup of tea since I was brought to that wretched place."

Burchardt angrily freed the samovar from its niche in the bar, spilling hot tea on his pants. He cursed under his breath.

She laughed at his clumsiness. "I'll take one sugar," she said, gazing out the window.

He gave her the tea. Then he poured himself a cup of straight vodka.

Down the block, Goering, Kurdorf, and the two young men sat in an ancient Mercedes. The young men were checking their weapons, which were identical to Goering's.

The Rolls pulled away from the asylum, then turned the corner. Goering made no move to start the car.

"Shouldn't we be following them?" Kurdorf asked.

Goering shook his head and sighed. "All in good time. The streets are empty. We'll have no trouble."

The calm in Goering's voice impressed Kurdorf.

Curt Zyklon drove the Rolls carefully along the ice-slicked streets. He wasn't sure where they were going, but presumed they were not staying in Paris since the old man had already checked them out of their hotel. So he headed east, toward Germany, wishing he were already home, warm and comfortable in bed beside his wife.

Burchardt chuckled as Curt nosed the Rolls up the Avenue Jean-Jaurès. "Are you homesick, Curt?" he asked, sliding open the partition.

"Sir?"

"We seem to be leaving Paris in the general direction of the German border."

Curt was flustered. Did the old man want to stay? "I thought that—"

"It's all right, Curt. You're absolutely right. We are going home. But it's late and we're all tired. I've made arrangements for us to stop at a hotel in Reims. You know the way, no?"

Curt had diligently studied the road maps before driving to Paris. "Yes, sir."

"Fine. Then onward to Reims." Burchardt felt almost giddy; everything had gone so smoothly. Even his anger with the woman had subsided. She had said nothing more, made no further demands. Staring out the window, watching the beautiful white-stoned buildings flash by, she sipped her tea, her pinkie daintily extended.

Burchardt finished his drink. Tempted to refill his cup, he decided against it. He didn't want to fog up his mind, at least not until they reached Reims.

They were now at the outskirts of the city. A bell clanged somewhere up ahead. Burchardt leaned forward. "What is it, Curt?"

"A railroad crossing. There must be a train coming through soon."

Burchardt rolled down his window. The area looked industrial, empty at this hour of the morning. Not a good place to stay.

"Don't wait," Burchardt said.

The black and white crossing gate started to descend.

"Sir, I think—"

"I told you to go!"

"Yes, sir." Curt floored the gas pedal. The Rolls lurched forward and bounced over the tracks, barely clearing the wooden gate as it came down and blocked the road.

* * *

"We're going to lose them," Kurdorf said.

The Mercedes edged up to the crossing gate. A train whistle screeched down the tracks.

"Shut up!" Goering said, shoving the gear shift into reverse and moving the car ten yards back from the gate. The train was approaching from the right, steam from the locomotive rising high into the night sky. Kurdorf figured it would roar through the crossing in about twenty seconds.

Goering suddenly jammed down on the gas pedal and drove straight toward the gate.

Somehow Kurdorf held back a scream as the Mercedes split through the first barricade, jostled over the tracks and rammed through the gate on the other side. A long plank of wood bounced off the hood. The Mercedes cleared the train by ten feet.

"Somehow I don't think you're cut out for this sort of thing, Kurdorf," said Goering, turning then to the two men in the back. "Get ready—we're going to take them."

Burchardt was about to apologize to Curt for his outburst when a spear of light cut through the rear window of the Rolls. A car was keeping pace about fifty yards behind. "Hurry, Curt," Burchardt said. "We're being followed." The girl remained silent, her hands in her lap, as calm as if she were taking a leisurely tour of the French countryside.

Curt wrestled the steering wheel to the right as the Rolls swerved on the icy road. In the rear view mirror, he could see the car quickly cutting the distance between them.

"Faster," Burchardt ordered.

The Rolls spurted ahead, gaining ground, its superbly crafted engine giving it a powerful advantage over the other vehicle. Tiny crystals of snow melted on the windshield and hailstones rattled against the Rolls's hood and roof. Curt glanced in the mirror, saw no sign of the pursuing car.

"I think they're gone," he said.

"Maybe they weren't following us at all," said Burchardt. "But it's always better to be safe than—"

The Rolls, streaking along the road at seventy miles per hour, suddenly hit a long patch of ice and began to slide, its back wheels whipping to the right. The car flew off the road and careened down a hill that leveled out along a frozen stream.

Wrestling with the wheel, Curt managed to turn the Rolls away from the stream. The back wheels sank into a shallow, watery ditch. As Curt gunned the engine, the back wheels spun dizzily and spit up shards of cracked ice. The Rolls went nowhere.

Curt stepped on the clutch and threw the car into reverse. The Rolls jerked back, still mired in the ditch. Burchardt helped the girl up from the floor of the car. "Are you all right?"

"I . . . I think so."

Lights from a car on the road suddenly bathed the Rolls, momentarily blinding Burchardt. Curt, a hand shielding his eyes, shouldered open the door.

"Stay here, Curt," Burchardt said, his vision clearing in time to see his driver outside the Rolls, scrambling for the gun inside his coat. "No," screamed Burchardt. "Put it away!"

Shots exploded in the air, five shots fired from above them, but none by Curt. The chauffeur slammed against the side of the Rolls, then pitched to the ground, blood spilling from his chest.

"Oh, my God," Burchardt said. "Oh, my God."

Four men came down the hill. The first two were young and armed with pistols. Burchardt noticed that they were identically dressed: gray coats, brown shirts, and dark slacks tucked into knee-high black boots. Behind them came a man wearing a long suede coat. At his side was a shorter, middle-aged man trying desperately to keep his glasses from bouncing off his face.

Goering leaned into the open front door. "Your driver is dead. My men are armed. I want you and the girl to come out slowly. And please—no foolish heroics."

Burchardt came out first. The girl hesitated, then followed. Her haggard looks disappointed Goering, who was expecting someone more regal.

"I have money," Burchardt said, his voice quivering with fear. "I can pay you."

Kurdorf felt as though he were going to be sick to his

stomach. He was sure that there were to be no witnesses. He stared stupidly at the bloody, twisted body of the driver, surprised that one man could bleed so much. He reached into the car and switched off the lights. The man's body faded into the darkness.

Goering told the young men to escort the girl to the Mercedes. Kurdorf gathered up the luggage from the floor of the Rolls and started up the hill.

The girl was struggling fiercely as the two men forced her into the Mercedes. Kurdorf followed them, trying to resist the temptation to turn around. Unable to stop, he turned just as one final shot cracked out.

Goering, his pistol pointing to the ground, stood over Burchardt's body. Most of Burchardt's head was gone.

The girl screamed. Goering pocketed his gun, trooped past Kurdorf. "Get a shovel out of the trunk," Goering said. "But first bring up those bags."

Dazed, Kurdorf obeyed. He traded the suitcases for a shovel. One of the young men, also carrying a shovel, led him down the hill to the side of the stream, where they started digging into the hard earth. Kurdorf's wheezes grew louder.

"That's enough," Goering said after they had dug a hole three feet deep. "We don't have time for a proper burial."

They dropped the bodies into the hole. Blood from the chauffeur stained the side of Kurdorf's coat. They shoveled dirt and mud over the bodies.

Goering was kneeling next to the Rolls, wiping blood from its mirror-like fender. "That's enough of that. Now help me push the car out of here."

Enough, thought Kurdorf. Forget the car. Leave it here or drive it into the water, but let it be.

As if he had read Kurdorf's mind, Goering said: "We'll sell the car in Paris. She's worth too much to leave here." He sounded sincere, but Kurdorf didn't believe him. Kurdorf felt that Goering wanted the car for himself.

Kurdorf and the young man, whose name was Dietrich, moved behind the Rolls while Goering manned the steering wheel. "All right," Goering said, thrusting the car into gear. "Give it a good push."

The back wheels spun in the shallows, drenching Kurdorf

and Dietrich as they rocked the car back and forth. Finally, the limousine broke free and shot up the hill to the road.

Goering stopped the Rolls and got out. "Dietrich, I want you to follow us back to Paris. Whatever you do, don't crash it. It has a far greater value to me than you do."

Kurdorf followed Dietrich up the hill. He sat next to Anastasia in the back seat of the Mercedes. She was bunched in a corner, crying. The other young man, whose name Kurdorf didn't know, sat in the front seat, his gun trained on the girl.

Kurdorf heard Goering slam shut the trunk of the Mercedes. Then Goering slid one of Anastasia's suitcases across the front seat and sat behind the steering wheel.

"Let's see if we've wasted our time," he said, opening the valise.

Kurdorf leaned forward, watching intently. He had nearly forgotten about the documents, forgotten their importance to the mission. He watched Goering take out two expensive-looking books, a pack of letters tied by a single blue ribbon, and a large envelope filled with photographs. Goering sifted through the bottom of the bag.

"It's here," Goering said triumphantly. "Everything is here." He replaced the documents and shut the bag.

Despite himself, Kurdorf felt elated. The killings had confused and troubled him. But now they had the papers. He thought about the mission and what its success could mean to him and his comrades in Munich.

Goering twisted the key in the ignition and the Mercedes coughed, shook, and finally started up. Goering steered the car back onto the road. The Rolls trailed discreetly behind, an unlikely companion to the scarred and dented Mercedes.

The girl in the back seat suddenly sat up, wiping away her tears.

"You cannot do this to me," she said. "I am the Grand Duchess Anastasia Nicolaevna."

"Keep quiet," Goering said. "We know who you are. We can do anything we want. You will do as we tell you."

The girl said nothing. Kurdorf admired Goering's ability to command respect from a daughter of the Czar. He wished he was like Goering—imposing, authoritative, a leader. He felt an asthma attack coming on. He tried not to wheeze. He noticed that the blood on his coat had already dried.

CHAPTER 3

Ernest sat alone at a table in the bar of the Palace Hotel in Lausanne, Switzerland. Yawning, he began to write his sixth cable of the night for William Randolph Hearst.

PASHA INSWARDS UNHARMED
SMYRNA BLAME GREEKS

Not bad, he thought, but not great either. There was a guy on the *Baltimore Sun* named Hodgeson who wrote the fastest and best cables in the world.

This one wasn't in Hodgeson's class, but it was good enough. He reread the sentence. Yes, definitely good enough for Hearst's editors, who would translate it as:

"Ishmet Pasha in an exclusive interview with the correspondent of the International News Service (PASHA INSWARDS) denied that the Turkish forces had committed atrocities in Smyrna (UNHARMED SMYRNA). The city, Pasha declared, was sacked by troops of the Greek rear guard before the first Turkish patrols entered the city (BLAME GREEKS)."

Cablese made sense since each word cost about three dollars to send to America. Even Citizen Hearst, the doyen of the Fourth Estate, wouldn't part with that kind of dough to cable an entire story. So cablese was the style. It was okay, sort of challenging and fun since it taught you to use words economically. But the fun was quickly wearing thin for Ernest; for six straight days—ever since he'd arrived from Paris—he had been running the wires from the Lausanne Peace Conference for Hearst's two services, International News and Universal. His job was to wire stories to America from nine in the morning to midnight. Last night, he had nearly fallen asleep on his feet as he trudged up the sloping, slippery hill from the Chateau Ouchy—where the conference was being held—to his grungy hotel on the Avenue de Georgette. Only the snow whipping into his face kept him awake. When he got to his room, he had been too exhausted to take off his clothes.

He wrote another bit of cablese, then pushed the pad away. William Randolph Hearst would just have to wait. And besides, who gives a damn about some territorial dispute between the Greeks and Turks? They probably don't even care, Ernest thought.

A day-old copy of the Paris edition of the *New York Herald* lay on the seat next to him. He glanced at the front page. Marshal Foch was threatening to invade Germany unless war reparations were paid. In Washington, the Harding administration was still considering the proposed merger of the Armour and Morris meat packing firms. And in New Jersey, a grand jury had refused to indict Frances Stevens Hall in the murder of her husband, the Rev. Edward Wheeler Hall, and his choir singer, Mrs. Eleanor Mills. "Their bodies," the paper said, "were found ten weeks ago beneath the famous crabapple tree."

Great stuff, Ernest thought, putting down the paper. He surveyed the three-deep bar through the smoky haze. The Palace Bar was quite elegant—all dark wood paneling, glass-top tables and bartenders fluent in at least three languages. The place was custom-made for the wily Swiss bankers who frequented it at lunch and after work. Ordinarily, the bar closed at midnight, its daytime and evening customers safely tucked away in bed, dreaming pleasantly of sound currencies. But now the joint was jumping, thanks entirely to the peace conference. Diplomats, journalists, bureaucrats, and spies drank champagne, smoked malodorous cigarettes, cracked bad jokes and tried to make up for the boring hours spent sitting solemnly in the Chateau Ouchy, listening to the Greeks harangue the Turks and the Turks harangue the Greeks. Scattered through the crowd, Ernest noticed, were a number of ladies of the night. Their presence might make a good sidebar story, he thought.

Sara Morgan, the correspondent for the Allied News Service, came into the bar. He watched with interest as Sara threaded her way through the crowd, grinning at certain so-called dignitaries, ignoring others, stopping once or twice to actually honor a lucky individual with a few words. She always talked to the most important, the most influential man in the group. She finally extricated herself from the clutches of a lecherous French diplomat and joined Ernest at the table.

"God, what a bunch of pathetic farts," she said, wiggling out of her coat. Ernest always had to remind himself that he was married whenever he was around Sara Morgan.

"Why bother with them?"

"Sources, Ernest, sources. Did you know, for instance, that Mussolini's bowels have been bothering him and he's having his own personal physician brought up here?"

"I missed that somehow. But it doesn't matter—how would I put 'bowels have been bothering him' into cablese?"

"You wouldn't have that worry if you came to work for Allied." Catching a waiter's attention, she held up Ernest's empty beer glass and signaled for two more lagers.

"Let's not get into that again," Ernest said.

"They're going to want an answer soon."

Ernest had met Sara nearly five months earlier at the Brasserie Lipp. Over a few drinks at the bar, Ernest regaled her with a string of stories. He'd also talked about writing. Sara, impressed by his good looks, agreed to read some of his clips, stuff he'd done for the *Toronto Star*. Impressed by the clips she'd sent them to her father, who was managing editor of the Allied News Wire. Morgan cabled back a job offer for Ernest, an offer that would mean moving back to America. But neither Ernest nor Hadley really wanted that.

Also, Ernest wasn't all that interested in newspaper reporting. He wanted to write short stories and novels. Paris, he felt, was a wonderful place to perfect his craft.

But Allied's offer was so damn tempting. The money was twice as much as he'd ever earned and the future was promising. On freezing cold nights, when the coals had run out and money was low, Ernest seriously considered taking the job. So far, however, he had stallen.

"Let me think about it some more," Ernest said.

"How much time do you need?"

"I like Paris. So does Hadley."

Sara, whose attempts to bed Ernest had so far been unsuccessful, winced at the mention of his wife. "It's your decision—not hers. A good writer can work anywhere—Paris,

New York, Omaha, a treetop in the Yucatan. It doesn't make a difference."

"Paris is a hell of a better place to write than Omaha."

"How do you know? Ever been there?" The waiter plunked down their drinks. "I covered a railroad strike there four years ago and I wrote just as well as I ever did in gay Paree. You just haven't been around."

"I was reporting before you even got out of grade school."

"A flattering exaggeration since I'm older than you. When did you get your first newspaper job?"

"Let me think . . . September . . . no, October, 1917. The *Kansas City Star* hired me."

"Big deal, you beat me by six months," said Sara. "Do you remember your first story?"

Ernest knew exactly what Sara was up to. One of the more appealing sides of newspaper work was the camaraderie among reporters. Newspaper people were great company, great drinking companions, great bullshit artists. You could never have just one drink when the press was around. Now Sara was trying to be one of the boys, lull Ernest into a sense of false security, convince him that she wasn't interested in romance.

Knowing all that, Ernest still played along. Remembering his early days as a reporter somehow made him feel better, made it easier to accept his current, exhausting plight. "Of course I remember it. Know why? Because I didn't know what the hell I was doing. I'd never been inside a city room before but that didn't faze me a bit. I was cocky—"

"Not you, Ernest! Never!"

"You want to hear this story or not?"

"I'm all ears."

"The city editor palmed me off on one of his assistants, a fellow named Wellington. Wellington tells me that the only reason I was hired is because the draft has taken away so many of their staffers. At this point, I'm beginning to get the picture, figure maybe I'm not going to become the ace reporter on the paper by the end of the day. Wellington showed me to a desk and then gave me an assignment. I'm to go to City Hall and cover the swearing in of twenty-three new citizens. Sounded easy. Before I left, he tells me to pay special attention in case any Krauts were turning American. If he hadn't told me, I never would have thought of it."

"God, you were green."

"Greener than an Irishman's brogue. So, I went to City Hall. I covered this earth-shattering event. There were no Krauts, just a bunch of Poles and Italians. I got back to the office and Wellington bawled me out for not calling him. I'll never forget it. 'Mr. Hemingway,' he said, 'always keep in touch with the city desk. Consider the telephone your umbilical cord.'"

"He sounds like my father."

"Well, he was right. He knew I had a lot to learn. After that he told me that the first edition deadline was three P.M. I had an hour to write a two-take story. No problem, right?"

"Lots of time."

"Sure. But not for me, not then. What was amazing was that at this point I still hadn't realized that I had no real idea how to write a news story. So I started humming—which next to whistling is the worst possible thing you can do in a newspaper office—and feeding my typewriter with paper. Then my mind went blank. I couldn't think of a thing to write. Nothing. I tried a few leads. They were terrible. Like: 'The population of the United States increased by twenty-three yesterday as fourteen Italian and nine Polish immigrants pledged allegiance to the red, white, and blue.'"

Sara giggled. "That's awful."

"Be charitable—I was only eighteen and nervous. By now I was beginning to think maybe I'm not such a hotshot. Sweat was pouring out of me. I had all of ten minutes until deadline. Wellington kept sneaking glances at me. Finally, I got an idea. I filled out a library slip and had a copyboy get the clips on citizenship. I spilled the clips on my desk and found one written three years earlier about a swearing-in ceremony similar to the one I had just covered. I copied it, changing the appropriate facts. Just to salve my conscience, I added a few flourishes of my own. Then I handed it in, right on time."

"What happened?"

"I waited. Five minutes. Ten. Finally, Wellington called me to his desk. 'Not bad,' he said. 'But in the future, let's do without the poetic touches.' Then he handed me my story. Everything was the same except for the five sentences I'd added. Wellington had penciled them all out."

Sara's laugh was as dry as vermouth.

"It wasn't funny. I was devastated. Then Wellington opened

his desk drawer and gave me a copy of the *Star's* stylebook. 'Make it your bible,' he said. I took his advice, read the book religiously and learned how to write a news story. It took a little longer than I'd anticipated, but in four months' time I was one of the aces of the staff."

"Modest as ever," Sara said.

Ernest shrugged, deciding not to tell her just how much influence the *Star's* stylebook, with its emphasis on simple, unadorned sentences, had had on his fiction, too. Sara had little faith in any prose not set under an eight-column headline.

"That's really a wonderful story," she said, quaffing her beer. "One day I'll tell you about my first day on the job. It's not as funny but it is more erotic."

Ernest lowered his gaze from her face. "Why don't you ever wear a brassiere?"

"I hate them. And in case you haven't noticed, I don't need one. Does your wife?"

"Be nice. I know it's difficult but try."

She pouted, an expression she'd perfected to an art. "We get on so well together. It's a shame you're dedicated to the idea of monogamy."

"It's not easy when you're around."

"That's probably the nicest thing you've ever said to me."

Ernest wiped a line of beer suds from his upper lip. A certain feeling of light-headedness was creeping into his brain, a dangerous condition with Sara so close at hand. "Lucky for me all I get at my hotel is cold showers."

"Then let's go to mine. There's plenty of hot water, even in the bidet."

Ernest chuckled. "Why is it that every time I talk to you I feel the need to go to confession?"

"I'm glad to see I'm having such a good influence on you," she said, swinging around in her chair to study the crowd at the bar. "Christ, will you look at that lug."

The bar was its usual crowded international stewpot. "Which lug are you talking about?"

Sara pointed to the far end of the bar where a tall, rough-looking man stood alone, drinking beer. Ernest recognized him as the bodyguard of Ishmet Pasha, the Turkish general.

"I wonder if he has his guns with him—he's never without them." She rose out of her seat and peered at the Turk. "By God, he does. All four of them—under his jacket." Sara sat back and scavenged through her purse. "Something has to be done," she said, her voice trembling with conviction. "This is a civilized place—not Dodge City."

"We could always poison his beer."

"He looks like he was weaned on the stuff. By now he's immune." Whatever she was looking for had so far eluded her.

"How about a little piano wire around his neck?" Ernest suggested, miming his own strangling by bulging open his eyes and sticking out his tongue.

"Never work. There's not enough piano wire in Lausanne to go around that thick neck. No, this calls for true inspiration." She stopped rummaging through her purse and, with the flourish of a magician, produced two cigars. *"Voilà."*

"Cigars?"

"Not just any cigars. These have certain . . . certain explosive properties."

"Who's going to give it to him?"

"One of us," she said.

"Since there's just you and me at this table I take it you mean that I'll be presenting our huge Turkish friend with the stogy."

"Don't be so typically masculine. I said one of us. We'll flip a coin. Loser does the dirty deed."

She reopened her purse and took out a Swiss coin about the size of an American half-dollar. She angled the coin under the light. "You want to call it?"

"Sure."

"Go ahead," she said, placing the coin on her thumbnail and flipping it into the air.

"Heads."

Deftly, she caught the coin, opened her hand. "You lose," she said, moving the cigars across the table.

"Why two cigars?"

"The other's for you," she said. "In case you choose suicide rather than face that bastard's wrath."

Ernest pocketed the cigars. "I bet you think I won't go through with this."

"My image of you would be shattered if you didn't. But there is one thing you should know."

"What's that?"

"Turks have no sense of humor."

"You're very encouraging." Ernest stood up. "You could have worked wonders with the Light Brigade." He walked through the crowd and sidled up to the Turk, craning his neck to look into the man's face. Ernest called over the bartender and ordered a whiskey.

The giant grumbled something to the bartender. The language was guttural and primitive. Probably what the cavemen spoke, Ernest thought. Whatever the Turk said was understood by the bartender, who promptly served up another brew.

Ernest could feel Sara watching him, waiting for his move. He stroked his moustache, a nervous habit. Nothing to be nervous about. With any luck this son of a bitch will put me out of my misery with one clean shot, Ernest thought, then remembered that he'd never seen a Turk do anything cleanly.

A strange odor seemed to be coming from him, and Ernest recognized it right away. The man smelled like a goat.

Turning to the Turk, Ernest offered him a cigar.

The giant appeared startled at first, then smiled at Ernest's generosity. Nearly all of the Turk's teeth were gold. Ernest wondered how many Greeks had been killed to pay for the dental work.

The Turk presented Ernest with a cigarette in return, then dipped his right hand inside his jacket, searching for a match. The cigarette smelled like camel turds and probably tasted worse. Glimpsing the guns strapped tightly against the man's waist, Ernest hoped that Sara was wrong about the Turkish sense of humor.

As the Turk struck the match and brought it up to the cigar, now clenched tightly between his gleaming teeth, Ernest instinctively began to back away. He bumped into someone, turned to apologize, then realized that the entire bar was quiet and everyone was looking at the Turk. Sara, who was standing on a chair for a better view, had obviously spread the word.

The Turk lit the cigar and puffed contentedly several times. Ernest wondered if Sara had mistakenly given him a perfectly good stogy or—

It was not a very loud explosion, and had the bar not been silent, no one would have noticed. But in absolute silence, it sounded like a goddamn howitzer.

The Turk, the billowing stump of the cigar still rooted in

his mouth, whirled around and his arms plunged into his jacket and in seconds all four guns were out—two on the bar top and one clamped in each hand and both aimed at Ernest.

Customers at the bar backed off. Several ran out of the hotel. Convinced that he was about to die, Ernest started to laugh, a maniacal roar that he hoped would prove contagious.

Miraculously, it did.

The Turk spit out the cigar and laughed. The crowd let out a collective breath, joining in the laughter. The Turk insisted in pidgin English that Ernest have a drink. "I like you," he said. "You got balls." Happy still to be capable of drinking, Ernest drank with the Turk.

For ten minutes he listened attentively to the Turk, pretending to understand at least every other word. Finally, the Turk pointed to the clock behind the bar, grunted what Ernest presumed was goodbye and departed.

"A commendable achievement," said Sara, toasting Ernest with her drink.

"Something for my memoirs." Ernest sat down.

"Look who just came in," Sara said. "It's Marcos, the Greek ambassador."

"Big deal."

Sara stood and smoothed down her skirt. She took a pen and notebook from her purse. "Maybe we can get together later," she said.

"Where are you going?"

"To interview Marcos."

"He doesn't talk to the press."

"He talks to me."

"I'll bet he does." Ernest watched her head for Marcos's table. She had the most subtly provocative walk he'd ever seen. Lead us not into temptation, he thought and wished Hadley were with him.

Why shouldn't she be?

There was only one good reason: they couldn't really afford the train fare. But he felt too lonely to care about their economy.

Ripping off the top page of his cable pad, he started to write to Hadley. He wanted her to come to Lausanne.

CHAPTER 4

In the smoky, overheated cellar of the Cafe Neumann in Munich, Germany, Adolf Hitler held his audience spellbound.

Clenched fists pounding the podium, Hitler screamed condemnation of the Treaty of Versailles, the Jews, the Bolsheviks, and any German who would not cast aside his own interests to help save the Fatherland.

"Only a dictatorship can save Germany," cried Hitler, his eyes ablaze with a furious passion.

The hundred men packed into the cellar roared approval. Hitler burrowed his hands in the pockets of his belted raincoat and nodded acknowledgment.

Standing impatiently near the back door, Goering wondered what Hitler's reaction would be to his idea—a slight, but, in his own opinion, quite brilliant variation on the original Anastasia plan.

Goering had few doubts about the idea. But he worried about Kurdorf, who was overseeing the operation in Paris while Goering consulted with Hitler in Munich. It had been nearly two weeks since the kidnapping. Goering expected that the Bolsheviks would agree to examine the Romanov documents very soon. Once that was done, and the Bolsheviks realized that Anastasia was genuine, Goering knew that they would agree to buy her.

What Goering feared was that the Bolsheviks would demand a meeting while he was still in Munich. He had no confidence in Kurdorf. Goering prayed that the Bolsheviks would make no move until he returned to Paris.

As Hitler's voice thundered through the cellar, his audience's excitement grew, their shouts of encouragement drowning out Hitler's final words. Finally, Hitler held up his hands in mock surrender and retreated from the crowd, shaking dozens of hands as he slowly approached Goering.

Opening the back door, Goering followed Hitler into the rain-slicked alley. "Excellent," said Goering.

"You thought so? I prefer speaking outdoors—the crowds are bigger and more responsive."

"Still, you were effective."

A chilling drizzle hastened their progress up the Ledererstrasse. After two blocks, Hitler led Goering into a nearby cafe. They sat in a back booth and ordered coffee.

"I'm pleased that your plan is working so well," Hitler said. "But I'm also very curious about your return to Munich. What's so important that you couldn't tell me by cable?"

Goering sipped his coffee, then took a deep breath. "I'd like to refine your plan—add a twist that will bring in even more money for the party."

"Of course we need a great deal of money to expand. But I don't want anything to jeopardize any deal we might make with the Bolsheviks. They're the ones who will pay for Anastasia."

"This jeopardizes nothing. But it's possible that we can double our payment and, at the same time, discredit the Bolsheviks."

Hitler, who despised the Bolsheviks, had taken weeks to approve Goering's original proposal. He hated the idea of doing business with the Bolsheviks. Therefore, Goering was certain that Hitler would endorse this new strategy, which would discredit them.

"You have my complete attention." Hitler pushed away his cup and laced his hands together as if in prayer.

"As you know, our plan now calls for the Bolsheviks to examine the Romanov documents—an examination we believe will convince them that Anastasia is real and is worth buying from us. It's a good bet that once they have her they will secretly liquidate her—it wouldn't say much for Bolshevik efficiency if the world was to learn that somehow they had failed to execute all of the Czar's family four years ago."

"What do we care what they do to her? A Romanov may not be a Bolshevik but she's still a Russian."

"But there are others who are also interested in our royal princess, others who will pay us well."

"Who?"

"The White Russians."

"You propose to sell her to the Whites as well?"

"Exactly. The Whites are desperate for a leader, someone to unite them. If they are ever to defeat the Bolsheviks—and the Whites still believe they can—then they must have someone to inspire them. Who better to accomplish that than the sole surviving child of Nicholas and Alexandra?"

"Nicholas and Alexandra had no twin daughters. How do you deliver one Anastasia to two different sides?"

"By not delivering her to either one."

The waiter approached to refill their cups. Hitler waved him away. "How do you do that?"

"Once both the Bolsheviks and the Whites have paid us, Anastasia will die, just before she is to be turned over to either side. We'll tell the Bolsheviks that she tried to escape and was shot. They shouldn't be unhappy—we'll be doing them a favor."

"And what do we tell the Whites?"

"We accuse the Bolsheviks of the cold-blooded murder of the Grand Duchess. Perhaps we'll show the Whites her bullet-riddled corpse. The Bolsheviks will, of course, deny it—but no one will believe them. The rest of the world views them as savages. Such a murder fits right into their pattern. After all, they executed the rest of the Romanovs. Think what the Whites will do—a poor, defenseless girl slaughtered by the merciless Reds."

"There's just one problem."

"What's that?" asked Goering, anticipating Hitler's question.

"If the Bolsheviks are given the Romanov documents, how do we convince the Whites that the girl really is Anastasia? What do we show the Whites?"

"We divide the documents—half to the Bolsheviks and half to the Whites."

Hitler examined his hands for a full minute. "It's brilliant," he said finally. "Do what you must."

"I won't disappoint you."

"I know that. But you'd better wire Kurdorf and tell him to reserve half the documents in the event the Bolsheviks approach him in your absence."

"I'll do that immediately," lied Goering. There was no

need to contact Kurdorf; Goering had ordered him to set aside half the documents before leaving for Munich.

Hitler made no protest when Goering paid the bill. Outside, the rain had stopped. They walked along the Ledererstrasse. "I want you to know how honored we are to have you as a member in the party—"

Hitler silenced Goering's protests with a wave of his left hand. "Don't be modest. You're a hero, a patriot, a true German. Your presence adds an enormous amount of credibility to our cause."

"I'm the one who is honored."

Hitler suddenly stopped. More than two hundred people lined the sidewalk across the street. At first, Goering thought they might be waiting to get into a cinema; then he took a closer look down the block and saw that the line started at the imposing bronze doors of a bank. Made desperate by the monstrous inflation smothering Germany, the people were waiting for the bank to open in the morning so they could withdraw their meager savings.

"Poor bastards," said Goering.

Hitler walked down the line, stopping regularly to talk to a familiar face. Goering, who stayed at Hitler's side, knew that more people recognized him than Hitler. He wondered how long that would be the case.

Ten minutes later, Hitler and Goering reached the end of the line. As they headed toward party headquarters several blocks away, Goering shook his head in disgust. "They don't stand a chance."

"They'll have their chance." Hitler smiled.

Goering understood Hitler's smile. For without those people and hundreds of thousands like them across Germany, Goering knew that Adolf Hitler and the Nazi party would never gain power.

In a fourth-floor suite in the hotel George V, a young woman who called herself Renata Lande stretched contentedly in her bed, luxuriating in the powder-blue silk sheets that caressed her naked flesh.

The man next to her slowly pulled the covers away and

kissed her full breasts. Laughing, she pushed him away. "There isn't time, Sergei," she said, tousling his thick black hair with her hands. "Offenbach will be calling soon." Wrapping herself in the top sheet, she walked to a table near the bedroom door and opened her purse.

Her companion made no move to cover his nakedness. He was about twenty-five years old, with a muscular body and friendly, boyish face. "There's no guarantee that Offenbach will call," he said.

"He'll call. We paid him too much money for him to fail." She dug into her purse and took out a pack of cigarettes. "Have you seen my cigarette holder?"

Sergei patted the bed. "It's probably here somewhere. Why don't you come back and look for it."

"I can do without it." She lit a cigarette. She was a year or two younger than Sergei. Her hair was cut fashionably short, accenting her striking face. She had dark green eyes and a long, rather aristocratic nose. She crossed her arms, her right hand holding the cigarette, her left hand covering a thin scar that ran along her upper arm.

"You'll catch cold," said Sergei.

"What about you?" she asked, moving to the window which overlooked the Champs-Élysées. "At least I have a sheet on." She parted the curtains, and a wedge of gray December twilight cut across the room.

Sergei went into the bathroom. When he emerged a minute later with a towel around his waist, Renata was still at the window, staring at the traffic moving along the avenue.

"Are you all right?" he asked as his arms went around her.

"I don't like this waiting, this uncertainty. I wish we were back in Germany and everything was the way it had been."

"It will be," he said, kissing her neck. "I promise you that."

The phone rang, startling her. "It's Offenbach," said Sergei. "No one else knows we're here."

"Write everything down," she said as he went to answer the phone. "Get the most specific information you can."

As she listened to Sergei speak to Offenbach, she realized how much Sergei had improved his German. She snuffed out her cigarette in a cut-crystal ashtray. Sergei stopped writing and hung up.

"Well?" she asked.

Sergei read from the notes he'd taken. "The National Socialists have struck a deal with the Bolsheviks. They're going to deliver the Romanov documents to the Bolsheviks tomorrow morning at the Gare de Lyon."

"What time?"

"Seven."

"The station will be crowded then. Did he know who's bringing the papers?"

"No. But he said the courier will be coming alone, walking from the Left Bank. He'll cross the river at the Pont Austerlitz."

"Did Offenbach know where they're keeping Anna?"

"No. But he said he'd try to find out—for a price."

"Is he sure she's not involved in tomorrow's exchange?"

"He said only the Romanov papers were being brought. The Bolsheviks want to make sure Anna is genuine before buying her. Hence the documents. Offenbach said the Bolsheviks are paying five thousand dollars in American money just to examine the documents."

Renata unfolded a street map of Paris on the table. She traced the short distance from the bridge to the train station. "You'll have to stop him when he comes off the bridge and turns right."

"How will I know who he is?"

"Look for Anna's bag—the one she stored the documents in."

"There's no guarantee they kept Anna's case."

Renata sighed. "You're going to have to improvise. We know the man will be alone and that he'll be carrying a small suitcase—the documents are too bulky to put in a pocket. Ask him something in German. If he responds, odds are he's the man."

"What about Anna?"

"One thing at a time. First the documents, then Anna. If the Bolsheviks get the Romanov papers, Anna is as good as dead. And so is the cause."

"Where will you be tomorrow morning?"

"In the station. I might be able to spot a Bolshevik face or two. They might be able to lead us to Anna."

Sergei turned his back on her. She could sense his fear. Tomorrow would not be easy for him.

"We'll have dinner here," she said and walked in front of him. Letting the sheet fall to the floor, she placed her hands on his shoulders and kissed him. His arms encircled her. They fell onto the bed.

CHAPTER 5

Bruno Schmidt strode along the rue Buffon, his right hand clutching a small, black valise. Schmidt, a tall, sullen man, was far from a natural strider and there was an awkwardness to his gait. He was aware of this, but still he strode. He was entitled; today he was working for the party.

He paused near the Pont Austerlitz to get his bearings. The Seine lapped gently against the stone embankment of the bridge. A small barge chugged along the river, its funnel puffing rings of white smoke. Lamps atop the bridge glowed in the early morning light, their reflections winking in the Seine's murky green waters. A dark-skinned street cleaner came over the bridge, pushing a cart loaded with a variety of brooms.

Schmidt rested the valise on the ground and checked the piece of foolscap on which his directions were neatly printed. Satisfied that he was going the right way, he picked up the case and resumed his walk.

He had no idea what was in the case. He didn't want to know. It was enough that he had been told to deliver the valise to the third platform of the Gare de Lyon. Its contents weren't important to him. What was important was that finally he was away from the hell hole of a bakery where he worked in Munich, away from the fat Jew bastard who owned the shop. For the first time in his life, Schmidt felt that he was doing something of importance.

All Jews were pigs as far as he was concerned. He called them that under his breath as he labored endlessly near the sweltering ovens in the back. Pigs with easy jobs they didn't deserve. Pigs whose conspiracy had brought a depression to Germany.

Every payday he cursed the Jews. His meager salary was worthless in the marketplace—a month's pay couldn't buy one decent meal. He had to live in the storeroom behind the bakery, eating the unsold, three-day-old meat pies from the Jew baker.

It galled Schmidt to admit to himself that he owed his existence to a Jew. The Jews were evil. The Jews were destroying his country. The Jews must be stopped.

Thankfully, others shared his beliefs. Throughout Germany, but especially in Munich, activists were rising up to denounce the Jews. Street corner politicians were almost as prevalent as mark notes. And as those marks became more and more worthless, more Germans were beginning to listen to these prophets of a new order.

Schmidt had listened. And eventually he did more than that, he actually joined the ranks of the activists. When he was not working at the bakery, he labored for the cause, distributing handbills, pasting up posters, setting up chairs for meetings, trying to interest others in the need for change in Germany.

His dedication was appreciated. People trusted him. Otherwise, he wouldn't be in Paris now, engaged in such an important assignment.

Schmidt recalled a recent incident in Munich. He and a friend were putting up posters for a forthcoming rally. A middle-aged man approached them, studied the poster. Schmidt's friend asked the man if he were coming to the rally.

"I'm a Jew. I don't think I'd be welcomed."

"Don't you approve of our party's platform?"

"You and your people are a disgrace to Germany. Of course I don't approve."

Schmidt's friend just laughed. Schmidt saw nothing humorous in the exchange. He slapped the Jew in the face.

The Jew just stood there, Schmidt's palm outlined in red on his face. Then he hurried away.

Schmidt laughed. "Jews are cowards," he told his friend.

Smiling now at the memory, Schmidt crossed the Pont Austerlitz and turned onto the Quai de La Rapée. A young man—clean cut, impeccably dressed—was walking along the sidewalk across the street, heading in the same direction.

The young man crossed the street. "Excuse me," he said in German.

Schmidt stopped. The man was no more than twenty-five. Handsome. His smile relieved Schmidt's anxieties. "Yes?" Schmidt asked.

"I thought you might be German," the man said. "I need some directions and I don't speak French. And there's no one else around to ask."

Schmidt looked down the quai. It was deserted. He was rather surprised that a stranger could pick him out as German. Still, there was no harm in helping a countryman. "Where are you going?"

"The Gare de Lyon. I have a train to catch."

Schmidt's first reaction was to let the man walk along with him. After all, his destination also was the Gare de Lyon. But he had been told to go alone to the station. He intended to do just that. Pointing down the quai, he said: "See that clock tower to the left? Just walk—"

Schmidt did not immediately understand why he could no longer speak. Then a terrible pain shot through his belly and he looked down and saw that the nice-looking young man with the smile had driven a knife into his stomach.

The young man took the valise from Schmidt's hand. Schmidt gagged on his own blood, and his left arm grabbed the young man's neck, clutching the shirt collar and tearing it away. A small medal around the man's neck broke away.

As Bruno Schmidt slid dying to the ground, he realized that the medal was a Star of David. He had been killed by a Jew.

The rear windows in the taxi were stuck shut and the foul smell from the driver's cigar clogged the cab. Hadley, leaning against the luggage piled next to her in the back seat, coughed, hoping the driver would take the hint.

He didn't.

"Would you mind putting out your cigar? It's annoying."

The driver eyed her in the rear view mirror and grimaced.

"I think I may be ill," she lied.

Taking a final generous drag, he grudgingly mashed the tip of the cigar against the smudged dashboard.

"Thank you, monsieur," she said, pleased that she had been so bold. Ernest definitely had had an influence on her, particularly on her shyness. She detested scenes, even small ones; before she'd met him, she never would have made even as modest a demand as she just had.

Thinking of Ernest, her hand patted the smallest of the suitcases. Wanting to surprise him, she had packed all his writing—every one of his short stories and poems—into the brown canvas bag which bore the initials EMH, for Ernest Miller Hemingway.

He had written that Lincoln Steffens was in Lausanne and she knew that Steffens wanted to see more of Ernest's work. Now he would have the chance. She was sure Ernest would be pleased.

The taxi rattled to a stop in front of the Gare de Lyon and the driver reluctantly helped her with her bags. Despite the unpleasantness of the ride, she tipped him generously. He mumbled a *"merci"* tinged with just the proper amount of ambivalence to suggest that the tip fell short of his expectations.

Shaking her head, she searched for a porter to help her with the three overstuffed suitcases and the small valise.

A young, dark-complexioned man with curly hair—an Algerian, Hadley guessed—pushed a cart through the station's entrance. Hadley beckoned him and he placed her luggage on the cart. She told him her train, doled out another generous tip and went inside to buy her ticket.

She stopped just inside the cavernous station. A dozen pigeons—permanent residents of the vast station—glided from the steel girders supporting the triangular, glass roof. Below, hundreds of early morning travelers crisscrossed their way to their trains.

Several people were lined up ahead of her at the ticket counter. She checked her watch. Seven-fifty A.M. Twenty minutes until her train was scheduled to leave.

The prospect of going to Lausanne and being with Ernest thrilled her. It had been ten days since he'd left, four since he'd wired. A bad cold had kept her from leaving immediately. She couldn't wait to be with him again. Just thinking of him made her—

"Oui, madam?"

Awakened from her reverie, she stared into the wrinkled face of the ticket clerk. She bought her ticket, nodded when the clerk told her that her train was running a few minutes late.

With time to spare, Hadley bought a paper at the newsstand in the corner. At the station cafe, she purchased two bottles of spring water and a chocolate pastry that was just too tempting to ignore.

Tucking the paper under her arm and the bottles and pastry in her purse, she went looking for her luggage.

Sergei was amazed at his calm. Forty-five minutes had passed since he'd killed the man, then dropped the body in the Seine. After that, he'd run along the quai and sought sanctuary in a small cafe diagonally across from the Gare de Lyon. There, he expected his body to betray him, to break out in sweat, to overwhelm him with nausea.

Nothing like that happened.

Instead, he sat at a corner table, sipping a *café au lait* and wolfing down two *croissants*. He was stunned by his hunger, his cold-bloodedness. His feeling of exhilaration frightened him. It was as if the murder was an everyday occurrence, part of a typical day's work. He felt no remorse, no revulsion.

A handful of people sat in the cafe, some chatting, others eating breakfast and contemplating the day ahead. Sergei was sure no one had witnessed the murder. The sky was only now starting to lighten. The quai, which he could see from the window, was still shrouded in darkness. No one in the cafe was interested in him; he was just another traveler killing time until his train departed.

The small valise he had taken from the dead German sat on the floor between his feet. He reached down and brought it onto the table. It was made of black leather and shaped like a doctor's kit.

A waitress brought him another coffee. Sergei noticed that his hands were shaking, his heart pumping faster. His nerves of steel were apparently buckling. He sipped his coffee, then snapped open the bag.

The first thing he saw were sheets from a Munich newspaper. He stared at them, hesitating before taking them out of the bag. What if there was nothing else? What if the documents weren't there? What if he had killed a man for no reason at all?

Breathing deeply, he lifted the pages from the bag and spread them on the table. Then he put the bag in his lap and peered in.

Thank God! Everything looked in order. The Bible was there, along with several irreplaceable photographs. Under the pictures, he found the morocco-bound book, a place mark sticking up from a page near the middle. He removed the bag and reached in for the rest of the documents.

What he saw made him sick.

Where the rest of the documents should have been were more sheets from the Munich paper. Impossible! He clawed through the newspapers. There was nothing else in the bag.

A wave of nausea swept through him. The bastards, he thought. They had kept the most important documents for themselves.

He quickly returned the books and photos to the bag. He left some francs on the table and walked outside. A cold wind from the Seine blew across the street. He shivered, covering his open collar with his left hand, the small valise held tightly in his right.

Shaking from the cold, he hurried across the square and entered the Gare de Lyon to look for Renata.

Steam shooting up from the locomotive drifted along the crowded platform as Hadley and others rushed to the train. Even traveling was different from America; here, when people were in a hurry, they were graceful about it, not rambunctious like commuters back home. They had a sense of style which Hadley liked.

Her bags were neatly arranged outside the fourth car, just a few compartments from her own. Three feet away, she stopped.

Something was wrong.

A mistake had been made.

The three larger cases looked like hers, but where was the small brown canvas valise, the most important bag in the bunch?

Frightened, she examined the suitcases, recognizing a long

gash along the side of the largest bag. They were definitely hers.

But where was the small valise?

She told herself not to panic. That reassurance worked for a few minutes, during which she had the presence of mind to carry the three suitcases into her compartment. Then she climbed off the train and went searching for the porter who had delivered the bags. All around her, people were hustling along the platform, obstructing her view. She hurried toward the station entrance. The porter must still have her bag, she reasoned. He had just accidentally left it on his cart.

She found the Algerian in front of the station, stacking a dozen elegant pieces of luggage onto his cart.

"Excuse me," Hadley said to the porter. "I can't seem to find one of the suitcases I left with you."

The Algerian finished his labors and started to push the cart into the station. "Don't understand what you mean," he said in a fractured style of French that took Hadley—who spoke the textbook variety—an extra few seconds to translate.

"The small suitcase," she said. "It's not with the rest of my luggage." Her voice grew louder. She looked self-consciously around to see if anyone had noticed.

"I put all bags next to train," the porter said.

"But one is missing!" she shouted. This time a few passersby cocked their heads at the angry tenor of her voice.

The Algerian appeared confused, even scared. Who was this crazy woman who spoke terrible French and insisted on bothering him as he worked?

"Where is the bag?" screamed Hadley.

The Algerian stopped the cart alongside a Geneva-bound train. As he hefted the suitcases onto the car, he said: "I put everything where you wanted it. Maybe husband took bag."

"My husband is in Switzerland."

"Pardon," the porter said with a smirk. "I thought gentleman who gave me money was husband."

"What gentleman?"

"The man who helped me . . . helped me . . ." The porter completed the sentence by making a lifting motion with his arms.

"Did he speak to you?"

"No." The porter finished loading the luggage onto the train.

Hadley's patience was gone. "What did the man do after he tipped you?"

"He took the little bag and walked away."

"And you let him?" she asked incredulously.

The Algerian shook his head, not in response to Hadley's question but in disgust at her behavior. He walked off. Hadley trailed him through the crowd, catching him near the gate of the platform. She wrapped her hand around his right arm. "You have to help me find the man—the man who took the valise."

The porter roughly pushed Hadley away and backed off.

"Stop!" she shouted as he abandoned his cart and ran.

She jogged after him, bumping into people, apologizing, getting cursed at in a variety of languages, nearly tripping several times. Her face was flushed, her eyes welled with tears. Brushing the tears away, she stumbled out of the station.

The porter was gone.

Sergei walked into the front entrance of the Gare de Lyon. This was his first time in the station and he stopped, searching for the third platform where he was to meet Renata.

People brushed past him. He had to dodge one lunatic—a woman who ran out of the station. Spotting a sign directing him to Gates 1 to 5, he started off.

"That's my bag!" a woman shouted behind him.

Sergei picked up his pace, unsure if the woman was talking to him and unwilling to stop and find out.

"That's my bag!" Sergei looked over his shoulder. It was the woman who'd run out of the station. She was only a few feet away.

"There must be some mistake," Sergei said.

"There's no mistake—that's my suitcase." The woman moved to take it from him. He backed away, painfully aware that several railroad employees at Gate 3 were watching them.

"I assure you," said Sergei, holding the bag in front of him, "that this is not yours."

The woman studied the bag, then shook her head. "I'm sorry," she said and hurried away.

THE HEMINGWAY PAPERS 51

Sergei watched her climb the stairs to the stationmaster's office. Renata, radiant in a sable coat, appeared at his side.

"What was that all about?"

"I'm not sure," he said. "But something's wrong."

"What happened? Did you get the documents?"

Sergei led Renata away from the gate. "Only half. I don't know where the others are. But that woman—" He paused. "That woman thought this bag was hers."

"Perhaps she was the Bolshevik waiting for the Nazi courier. I was expecting a man. I never thought to look for a woman."

"Did you see anyone suspicious on the platform?"

"No one."

"There she is," said Sergei as the woman emerged from the stationmaster's office, ran down the stairs and through Gate 3, boarding a train that appeared ready to leave at any moment.

"Follow her," said Sergei. "She's involved in this somehow. We have to find the rest of the documents. We have to find Anna."

Renata did not hesitate. Walking quickly—but not quickly enough to draw attention to herself—she passed through the gate and stepped aboard the train.

Sergei went immediately to the stationmaster's office, a dreary room occupied by a dowdy-looking man standing behind a chest-high counter. The man was carefully filling in a long red-colored form.

"I'd like to report a missing suitcase," Sergei said.

"Not another!" said the man. "A woman just came in here with the same complaint."

"Don't tell me my wife was already here?"

The clerk studied the form. "Are you Monsieur Hemingway?"

Sergei nodded. "This is embarrassing."

"Your wife was just here," said the man, obviously relieved that he would not have to fill in a second report. "She said that if the bag is recovered we can deliver it to a bookstore called Shakespeare and Company on the rue l'Odéon. I'm just filling in the details."

"I'm sorry to have troubled you," said Sergei, backing out of the office.

From the second-floor balcony, Sergei overlooked the entire station. Platform 3 was empty, the train gone.

Who was this Hemingway? Sergei asked himself. And how were he and his wife involved with the Romanov documents and Anna's kidnapping?

Alone in her compartment, Hadley cried.

For just how long, she couldn't say. But when finally she stopped—at least for the moment—her eyes were sore and her throat ached from sobbing.

Why had she left the bags unattended? How could she have been so foolish? Why had she even brought Ernest's manuscripts with her?

She knew why, of course. She had wanted to surprise him.

Well, he'd certainly have one now.

A big, unpleasant surprise.

She remembered that a month ago he had frantically searched the apartment for one of his stories. When he couldn't find it, he'd screamed at her, accusing her of misplacing the story. She told him she hadn't touched the story.

He had yelled some more, then stormed out, only to return an hour later, manuscript in hand. He'd left it in the hotel room around the block. Embarrassed over losing his temper, he had apologized.

Hadley could forgive—but not forget—his anger. And that time she had done nothing wrong.

Now she had. And she was frightened. Those stories and poems were Ernest's life. Now they were gone.

And it was her fault.

She buried her face in her hands and started to cry again.

CHAPTER 6

Benito Mussolini scrunched up his pudgy face in a calculated mask of concentration, his tiny eyes seeming to disappear in a roll of cheeky fat. As photographers snapped his picture, he affected an air of nonchalance. He sat behind the large, horseshoe-shaped table in the ballroom of the Beau Rivage Hotel and read a book, never looking up as the flashbulbs of the Speed Graphic cameras popped like a twenty-one gun salute.

Sitting in the second row, his legs crossed, his notebook seesawing on the tip of his shoe, Ernest watched the frenzied scene and shook his head.

It was pure madness. In a few minutes, Mussolini would be starting the press conference. Everyone knew he would say nothing of importance. Yet when the press conference was over, everyone would file a story based on the fat Italian's utterances. Journalists make the insignificant significant, Ernest thought. Quite a life.

Ernest had heard Mussolini speak twice before and each time he'd walked away convinced that the Italian was a phony. Fascism disgusted Ernest. When Italy turned *fascismo*, he had felt betrayed. After all, he hadn't shed his blood during the war for Italy to become a fascist nation. It made him sick.

Italy, of course, was not the only nation in political turmoil. He had made a trip recently to Germany and he knew that that country, too, was ripe for a revolution.

He remembered a story someone had told him there. Several people in Cologne had been busily defacing a statue of Wilhelm II. When a policeman tried to intervene, more people gathered and soon the crowd turned on the cop and killed him.

The story had troubled Ernest. As had a bunch of fascist thugs in Munich who had formed something called the National Socialist party.

Nazis, they called themselves.

The Nazis blamed the Jews for everything—inflation, unemployment, Germany's defeat in the war. The Nazi movement was small. But, like the crowd in Cologne, it was growing.

Ernest was jostled from his political musings as more reporters elbowed their way into the packed ballroom. Cigarette smoke, nearly as thick as the morning fog over nearby Lake Geneva, filled the air. The din was awesome: reporters screaming and cursing and jockeying for a place near the front.

Through it all, Mussolini, dressed in his patented black shirt, gray trousers, and white spats, remained a study of indifference. Two burly henchmen stood behind him, making sure no one distracted their leader from his book.

The book intrigued Ernest far more than the prospect of the press conference. What the hell was the wop reading? Boccaccio? Dante? Sabatini? Ernest got up and inched through the mob, sidestepping the photographers, who were now kneeling before Mussolini like Catholics at Lourdes. He stretched over the table and walked behind Mussolini.

One of the guards turned, his hand reaching for the gun nesting in a holster belted around his hips. Ernest jangled a batch of press credentials before the bodyguard's face. "*Journalisimo*," he said, catching just a glimpse of Mussolini's book.

"Go away!" the guard said.

"Anything you want, amigo." Ernest saluted and went to the side of the room, his second-row seat usurped by Sara Morgan.

Someone tapped him on the shoulder. Ernest turned. It was Lincoln Steffens, the grand old man of muckraking, currently in Lausanne as a special correspondent for the International News Service. "I thought Mussolini bored you, Ernest."

"I was interested in his choice of reading matter."

"And?"

"Our friend Benito is enthralled by a French-English dictionary."

"Admirable—he's trying to improve himself."

"The only problem is he's reading it upside down."

Steffens was not chagrined. "Perhaps he speaks English and French when he's standing on his head." At that moment, a dour Italian diplomat rose and announced that the press conference would begin. A reverential hush settled on the room as Mussolini launched into his introductory remarks.

Ernest made a few cursory notes, then tuned Mussolini out. In less than an hour, Hadley would finally be in Lausanne. He had been looking forward to her arrival for days. Lausanne—even the job—would be more bearable with her by his side.

Leaning against the wall, Ernest sneaked a glimpse at Steffens, thinking how little the man resembled the two-fisted image of the crusading reporter, especially one who had boldly exposed political corruption in *The Shame of the Cities*. With his wire rim glasses, meticulously groomed moustache, and goatee, Steffens resembled the president of a small town bank; in fact, the head of the bank in Ernest's home town—Oak Park, Illinois—could have been Steffens's twin. The only difference was the banker had a full head of hair, while Steffens combed his thinning locks down over his forehead in a triangle, as if to make up for its rapidly disappearing condition.

Ernest had met Steffens the previous April in Genoa, where both were covering an international economic conference. Steffens had read some of Ernest's reporting and asked to see his fiction. Ernest showed him *My Old Man*, a short story about a crooked jockey and his son. Steffens thought the story excellent and sent it to *Cosmopolitan*, recommending that the magazine publish it.

Steffens now moved a step closer to Ernest. "Our friend is rather desultory today," he whispered.

"Sara Morgan says he has bowel problems."

"Probably from writing his speeches with his sphincter." Steffens pocketed his fountain pen and pad. "Have you heard anything from *Cosmopolitan* yet?"

"Not a word."

"There's nothing more infuriating for a writer than waiting. All kinds of terrible thoughts cross his mind. Was it any good? Did I make a major mistake somewhere? Is the editor laughing when he should be crying? Crying when he should be laughing? There has to be a better way."

"Let me know if you hear of one."

"Is Hadley coming this evening?"

"Her train gets in in forty-five minutes."

"Wonderful—she's a charming young woman. I'd like to go to the station with you."

Ernest almost said no; he hadn't seen Hadley for days and he wanted to be alone with her. But Steffens was a patron, a champion of his work. There weren't many like Steffens crowding into his corner. He thought of Clive Russet, remembering the scene in the Amateurs, and he wondered how often he would have to suck up to people who could help his career. Until you make it, he thought. "She'll be delighted to see you," Ernest said.

Ernest flipped open his notebook, not to write quotes but to doodle. He had inked in three dollar signs before he realized what he'd done. Was money really that important? Only if you didn't have it.

He looked across the room at Sara Morgan, who was speedily transcribing every one of Mussolini's words. Sara was a lifer—a lifelong reporter. So was Steffens. Ernest hoped he wasn't one, too. He wanted to tell Sara to forget the job with Allied. If only the salary weren't so tempting. If only he and Hadley didn't need the money. If only . . .

The press conference was reaching a hot-winded finale. Mussolini, his blubbery face pouring sweat, screamed: "No more questions!" and stomped out of the room. A bodyguard snatched up the French-English dictionary, following Mussolini.

"Disappointing performance," observed Steffens as he and Ernest squeezed out of the ballroom.

"Doesn't matter. I'll still have to file something."

"Based on that claptrap?"

"Claptrap is my specialty. I can see the headline now. 'Italian Fascist Says He Wants Peace.' They'll spell it s-e-z."

"Catchy."

"Like leprosy."

Sara Morgan joined them in the lobby.

"Wonderful news," she said. "I have it on good authority that a ninety-seven-year-old Swedish diplomat dropped dead here last night and his room's available."

Steffens, a bemused witness to Sara's attempts to seduce Ernest, chuckled.

"I already have a room," Ernest said.

"But not with me."

"I have a story to file."

"Don't be so bloody serious, Ernest. I was just joking. Even my father—who lives to indulge me—wouldn't let me stay in the Beau Rivage. It's too damn expensive." She was wearing her ever-popular fur coat. Her hair was pulled back tightly in a bun. As usual, she looked stunning.

"Did Ernest tell you that Hadley is coming tonight?"

"Once too many times six times ago," she said, reaching for Steffens's hand. "Maybe I should make a play for Lincoln here."

"I appreciate being the object of a proposition, my dear. But I don't think I'd live through the experience."

Sara kissed both men on the cheek. "I've got a story to file, too," she said and danced away. "Give my best to Hadley, Ernest."

"Remarkable girl," Steffens said. "My deepest respect for resisting her."

Ernest shrugged. "If Hadley weren't coming today . . ."

Steffens nodded understandingly. "I know what you mean."

Outside the Beau Rivage, Steffens donned a ridiculous Swiss mountain climber's hat. "A gift from a Swiss colleague," he explained sheepishly. Ernest had to restrain himself from laughing; the hat, combined with Steffens's conservative banker's garb, made Steffens look like the bastard son of Heidi and George Babbitt.

Together, they trudged up the snowy hill that ran from Lake Geneva to the heart of the city. Ernest wasn't wild about Lausanne. The lake was nice and the French Alps, which rose raggedly along the other side of the water, were impressive. But that was about it. The rest of the city was rather dull and its industry—banking, watchmaking, and diplomacy—bored Ernest totally.

"Why does so much Swiss architecture look as though it were inspired by the cuckoo clock?" asked Ernest.

"Switzerland doesn't appeal to you?"

"It's fine, especially the countryside. But it gets a little boring. Unlike the natives, my idea of a good time is not dipping pieces of bread into melted cheese."

Steffens's laughter turned into a sneezing fit and he fished through his pockets for a handkerchief. The funicular clattered up the hill and stopped for them, blue sparks flicking from the overhead cable. Steffens began to talk politics, a subject he discussed in a most entertaining way.

This time, however, Ernest wasn't interested. Instead, he thought about a short story he was planning to write. It was about a young man who, away from his wife, almost has an affair with another woman.

Lavrenti Pavlovich Beria sat in the cramped, windowless office in the cinema on the Boulevard St. Michel. The walls were decorated with pictures of movie actors and actresses, none of whom Beria recognized. The office belonged to the theater manager, a Russian immigrant of no particular political persuasion who had reluctantly agreed to let Beria use his office after Beria pointed out that the manager's aged parents lived in a tiny village near Tiflis. Tiflis and its environs, Beria told the manager, were under his jurisdiction.

"Old people are so fragile," Beria said.

The manager handed Beria the key to his office.

Beria had deliberately picked the cinema as the place to meet with the Germans; his orders were to stay away from the embassy and any Russian haunts in Paris. It had taken two hours of combing Cheka files to find the cinema manager. So far, the theater had served his needs perfectly.

Beria contemplated Kurdorf's impending visit. When the Germans had failed to deliver the documents that morning to the Gare de Lyon, Beria had been furious; he still was. But he had learned over the years to cloak his fury beneath a facade of calm—as disarming and deadly a weapon as the pistol he carried in his pocket at all times. A calm, pleasant appearance often confused your opponent, forced him to make a mistake.

There was a knock on the door. Beria stood. "Come in," he said in German, knowing it was Kurdorf.

The door slowly opened. "Where is Schmidt?" asked Kurdorf.

Beria smiled. "Where are the Romanov documents?"

"You have them. You took them from Schmidt." Kurdorf's voice quivered.

"Sit down."

Kurdorf stood in the middle of the office.

THE HEMINGWAY PAPERS 59

"Sit down," repeated Beria.

Kurdorf did not move. Beria reached under his desk and brought out a small valise. At first, Kurdorf thought it was Anastasia's case, the one Schmidt had taken to the Gare de Lyon. But that bag had been black with a silver buckle. This one was brown, its buckle badly tarnished. The initials EMH were etched onto the canvas.

"My man at Gate 3 in the station waited forty-five minutes. When your courier failed to appear, he saw this case and took it, even though it did not exactly fit the description he'd been given. But it was the only bag he saw that came close."

"It's not the case with the Romanov documents in it."

"We know." Beria opened the bag. "Take a look."

Kurdorf peered into the bag. A dozen blue-covered notebooks and several reams of typewritten paper were packed inside. "What is this?"

"Nothing as far as we're concerned. It's writing—fiction—by someone named Ernest Hemingway. He's an American journalist. Does the name mean anything to you?"

"No." Kurdorf reached in and took out one of the notebooks. Written on the cover was: Ernest Hemingway, 74, rue du Cardinal Lemoine.

"He's not there if you're thinking of visiting him. I've had his apartment searched. Nothing out of the ordinary."

"Where is he?"

"According to our sources, he's in Lausanne, covering that farce of a peace conference. I've ordered two of our best men to follow him but it's purely a precautionary gesture. I don't think he's involved."

Kurdorf dropped the notebook into the bag. "You still haven't told me what happened to Schmidt."

"Schmidt? Was he your courier?"

"Yes."

"I have no idea. As far as we know, your man never got to the station. In fact, as far as we know, there are no documents and you merely planned to steal five thousand dollars from us."

"I wouldn't be here if that were true. And how do I know you didn't eliminate Schmidt and take the documents to save yourself the money?" Kurdorf was proud of his observations.

"Because of this," said Beria, sliding open the top drawer on the desk and placing a stack of American bills next to the brown suitcase. "Here's the five thousand dollars. Our offer still stands. I wouldn't be meeting with you if I had the documents."

Kurdorf could not fault Beria's logic. But what had happened to Schmidt?

"Was your man reliable? Trustworthy?" asked Beria.

"Extremely. If he didn't arrive at the station, something happened to him along the way."

Beria returned the money to the drawer. "Then I suggest you find out what that something was. I've been ordered to tell you that you have just two days to produce the documents. Fail, and my superiors will write off your Anastasia as just another fake."

Kurdorf was momentarily tempted to tell Beria that half the Romanov documents had been held back, but he managed to keep that particular piece of intelligence to himself. "Do you need this?" he asked, tapping the brown case on the desk.

"No."

"I'd like to take it with me. I have superiors, too, and they'd like to know what happened this morning. It will be easier for me to explain your side of the story if I have something to show them."

"Take it—it's of no use to me."

Kurdorf nodded curtly, picked up the bag and opened the door.

"Two days," Beria said.

"I'll tell my people." Kurdorf exited.

Beria relaxed in the creaking chair behind the desk. He was damned if he was entirely certain what the Germans were up to. He considered ordering Strinsky and Proskumov off Hemingway. Despite what he'd told Kurdorf, he still was not convinced that Hemingway was merely an innocent bystander. Clearly, a third party was involved. As unlikely as it might seem, Hemingway could be that third party.

Beria knew that Kurdorf's superiors would also suspect Hemingway. He wondered what they would do next.

CHAPTER 7

The train steamed through the Lausanne station, sheets of snow slipping from the rounded sides of the huge black locomotive.

Ernest tapped the window of the station restaurant. Steffens nodded, quickly finished his whiskey-laced coffee and carefully folded up the restaurant's three-day-old copy of the Paris edition of the *New York Herald*.

As a cool wind blew up from Lake Geneva, Ernest stuck his chin deeper into the collar of the woolen coat. He leaned forward slightly, poised on the balls of his feet, waiting anxiously for Hadley to appear.

Steffens joined him on the platform as the first wave of passengers came off the train, many carrying skis and skates.

"I don't know why anyone would want to ski," Steffens said.

"Why not?"

"Besides being dangerous, it looks absolutely boring. Up the hill, down the hill like some kind of Alpine Sisyphus."

"I don't know about that."

"Have you ever done it?"

"Sure—it's great sport."

"That's the difference between youth and wisdom," Steffens said.

Only a few stragglers were left on the platform. For a sickening instant, Ernest thought Hadley had missed the train. Then he saw her stepping off, carrying two suitcases, putting them down, taking a third case from the hands of a helpful conductor. "There she is!" Ernest yelled.

As he hurried down the platform, he sensed something was

wrong. Hadley wasn't smiling, wasn't rushing to meet him. This wasn't like her.

"Hello, baby," he said, jumping over the suitcases and cradling her in his arms. "God, it's good to see you."

Hadley's arms went around his back. "Oh, Ernest, Ernest," she said. She was crying, muffling her sobs in the folds of his coat.

"What's wrong, baby? What's the matter?"

She pulled away from him, daintily wiping away the tears with the back of her hand. "I'm so sorry, Ernest. I've done something awful."

Ernest laughed. "What did you do? Forget your toothbrush?"

A slight smile contradicted her tears. "I wish that were it."

"Let's get going," said Ernest. "It's too cold out here." He scooped up two suitcases. Hadley took the third. By the time they reached Steffens, she'd stopped crying.

"Hello, my dear," Steffens took off his hat and bowed gallantly.

"Hello, Mr. Steffens."

"Hadley says she's done something awful," Ernest said. "I think she threw somebody off the train."

"Don't joke, Ernest. I'm serious."

Steffens put a hand on Ernest's arm. "Perhaps it would be better if I left the two of you alone and—"

"You'll stay right here with us," said Ernest, then turned angrily to Hadley. "I don't know what's gotten into you but Lincoln took time out from his schedule—his very busy schedule—to come down here and welcome you. This isn't a very nice way to return his hospitality."

Steffens was clearly embarrassed. "It's all right. I'll just—"

"It's not all right," Ernest said.

"I'm sorry, Mr. Steffens. I've been rude. It's just that I have something to tell Ernest and he doesn't seem to want to give me the chance to open my mouth."

"I understand, my dear. I'll just be on my way—"

"No, you won't!" Ernest boomed. "Whatever this cataclysmic announcement is, we'll all hear it. But we'll do it someplace where it's warm and we can all get a drink."

Both men looked at Hadley. "That will be fine," she said.

The only place nearby where it was warm and they could drink was the station restaurant. They took a table in the back. Ernest and Hadley ordered brandy. Steffens stayed with his spiked coffee.

"Okay, Hadley," Ernest said after the drinks arrived. "What is this catastrophic thing you've done?"

She sipped her brandy tentatively, then took several healthy measures. "I never wanted to hurt you," she said, her voice cracking with emotion.

Ernest reached across the table and patted her hand. He could tell now that she was serious, that she really felt she had committed some terrible sin. "Whatever happened couldn't be that bad. Nothing could."

She felt the tears about to start. "All I wanted to do was surprise you."

Ernest glanced exasperatedly at Steffens, then shifted his gaze to Hadley. "If I had a drum I'd roll it. The suspense is killing us. What happened?"

"Last night I decided I wanted to surprise you. I knew Mr. Steffens enjoyed *My Old Man* so I thought I'd pack all your stories and poems and bring them with me. That way you could show him some more of your work and do some revision. I put them all in the small valise your parents gave us. When I got to the Gare de Lyon, I gave everything to a porter and went to buy my ticket. When I got to the train, the luggage was on the platform—everything except the small valise."

Hadley stopped to gauge Ernest's reaction. He kept a poker face, eyes fixed on her.

"I went looking for the porter, found him, demanded to know what had happened to the suitcase. He said my husband had taken it—at least a man he presumed was my husband."

"Did he describe this man?"

"I didn't ask. I'm sorry."

"What happened next?"

Hadley took a deep breath. Her frail composure was crumbling. "I reported the theft to the stationmaster. Then I took the train and came here." She just got the last bit out before exploding into tears.

Ernest squeezed her hand reassuringly and made appropriate statements of comfort. "It's all right . . . really . . . I can rewrite that stuff . . . no problem." He was possessed by a combination of shock and anger. The stories couldn't be gone. It was impossible. He'd worked too hard for this to happen. Months of work, the hardest work he'd ever done. What the hell was Hadley trying to do to him? How could she have been so careless? What a goddamn stupid thing to have done. Incredible.

"Don't cry, baby," he said, knowing he didn't sound all that sincere. "We'll work it out."

Steffens offered Hadley his handkerchief and she dried her eyes and wiped away her sniffles. "There's no real reason for this remorse," he said. "All writers—good, bad, indifferent, barely literate—share a primordial fear that some dim-witted editor will one day lose their manuscripts. The result of all this fear was the creation of what is called the carbon copy. I'm sure Ernest made copies."

Carbons! Why hadn't he remembered? "Of course I did. I copied all my stuff. Did you pack the carbons, Hadley?"

"I'm not sure . . . I think so . . . maybe not."

Christ! Couldn't she get anything straight? "This is important, Hadley. Did you take them with you?"

"You don't have to talk down to me, Ernest—I know it's important." She tried to remember the moment when she opened the desk drawer and took out the manuscripts. She could picture the blue notebooks, the sheets of typing. But she couldn't be sure about the carbons. "I'm sorry, Ernest. I just don't know."

Ernest was about to lace into her, tell her that what she had done was stupid and careless and devastating. How could he ever recreate those stories? It had been difficult enough the first time around; no matter how hard he tried he could never rewrite them the same way, never improve them. It just couldn't be done. He felt as though someone had taken a knife, opened the scars on his legs and left him to die.

But he controlled himself. Yelling at Hadley would only hurt her and embarrass Steffens. So he reassured her that everything would be fine. Undoubtedly, the carbons were still in the apartment. "So there's nothing to get excited about," he said. He didn't really believe it and as he said it he wondered how much longer he could camouflage his anger with such insincere platitudes. Probably not much longer, knowing his temper.

A porter poked his head into the restaurant and announced that there was a taxi available. Taxis were rare in snowy

Lausanne, so both Steffens and Ernest jumped up and said they'd take it.

In the cab, Steffens pointed out a few places of interest in the town and entertained Hadley with stories about the peace conference. Ernest said nothing. He stared out the window, his right hand locked tightly in his left. He could think of nothing but the carbons. They had to be in Paris. *They had to be.* He had to go back and find out.

Ernest leaned forward. "When's the next train to Paris, driver?"

The man consulted his pocket watch. Ernest was surprised he had only one. "Two hours—at eleven-ten. The *Orient Express* comes through."

His bad luck was running high. The *Orient Express* was the most expensive train on the line; booking passage on it would put a crimp in their already paltry savings. But he couldn't wait. He had to get to Paris.

"You're not thinking of going back to Paris, are you?" asked Hadley.

"Yes, I am."

"I'll go with you."

"You just left. And we can't afford two tickets on the *Orient Express*."

Hadley protested, but Ernest was unwavering. Experience had taught him that it was much easier to travel alone. And he was angry with Hadley, angry enough to want to punish her. He wouldn't let her go back with him. It was a childish reaction but one which he couldn't deny.

The taxi jolted to a stop in front of Steffens's hotel.

"Let's have dinner tomorrow night, my dear," Steffens said. Then he shook Ernest's hand. "Good luck in Paris, son." Steffens eased out of the cab and enthusiastically joined several Italian reporters engaged in an animated discussion near the hotel's old-fashioned, gas-lit entrance.

"He's a very nice man," said Hadley, nestling closer to Ernest.

"The best." Ernest did not put his arms around her, did not kiss her, did not hold her hand. Instead, he continued to stare out the window, as if he were traveling through the chiaroscuro streets of Lausanne for the first time.

* * *

The suitcases made the winding climb up the narrow stairway to Ernest's room difficult. Twisting the ancient key into the squeaking lock, he shouldered open the door and turned on the overhead light.

Wedged into a frosted ice bucket on the night table was a bottle of champagne. Shit! He'd forgotten he'd ordered it to celebrate Hadley's arrival.

"Champagne! How lovely!" Hadley gushed. She lifted the dripping bottle out of the bucket.

"You can drink it all—I'm not in the mood." As soon as he said it, he was sorry; the pained look that crossed Hadley's face filled him with remorse. He knew he shouldn't say such things, knew they would have an effect on her. It was just that when he was angry, he couldn't control what he said.

"In that case, I don't want any either. I hate to drink alone."

"That's fine with me." He jerked the bottle out of the bucket and threw it across the room. The bottle smashed against the wall next to the window. The champagne rolled down the wall, leaving a large, explosive stain running to the floor in a dozen narrow rivers.

"For God's sake, Ernest, stop acting like a child!"

He was no longer angry. As she sat on the bed and cried, he moved next to her, holding her and stroking her hair. "I'm sorry, baby. It's just . . . I have to blow off a little steam sometime. I keep thinking about those stories—"

Hadley started to say something but Ernest put a finger to her lips. "It's not what you think. They may be gone forever and the thing that really bothers me is I don't know if they were any good. I think they were. Christ knows, I spent enough time working on them. For what? So a few people like Steffens could say they were good. They haven't been published—"

"They will be."

"Maybe. But there aren't any guarantees. Sometimes I wake up in the middle of the night and read some of them— stories I thought were first-rate when I wrote them. You know what happens? I read them and cringe. Who'd ever want to read that stuff? No one. Then other times I'll read them and decide that they're the best goddamn things anyone's ever written. Most of the time, I end up somewhere in between—just not sure what they are. So when you told me they were gone, I figured that's it, that's fate—forget it, it's not in the cards for me to be a writer."

Ernest had never been so open with her, so vulnerable. "You're not giving up," she said. "You're going back to Paris."

He smiled slightly. "I sure as hell have to do something."

"But what if the carbons are gone? What if you can't find the manuscripts?"

"Then I'll get drunk as hell, sleep it off, and come back and do my job."

"And when the conference is over?"

"I don't know. Maybe take the job with Allied."

He had written her of the offer with the news service, written so halfheartedly that she knew he wanted nothing to do with the job. But he had had his stories then. He had had hope that he would be able to write his way out of journalism.

She could always tell him that he was talking nonsense, that the job with Allied would be a waste of time, that he had to stick with his fiction, that his talent was great and one day he would succeed.

But he would expect such reassurances. He would dismiss them as nothing more than examples of wifely loyalty. So she said nothing. Instead she kissed him, gently at first, then harder, passionately. She unbuttoned his shirt and let her fingers dance across his chest. "I love this," she said, stretching out on the bed as he began to undress her. "And I love you."

CHAPTER 8

Sitting in the train station, Ernest brooded.

Normally, he would have been thrilled by the prospect of taking the *Orient Express*. The train's romantic history—he had read all about the spies, millionaires, aristocrats, sultans, and prime ministers who reportedly rode its gilded rails—appealed to his exaggerated sense of high adventure. Under better circumstances, he would have gone out of his way to get a good feature out of the trip for the *Toronto Star*. Wouldn't take more than an hour to bat out a story. Easy money.

But these weren't better circumstances. Preoccupied with the missing manuscripts, he tortured himself by remembering each story, each poem. He recalled plots, characters, dialogue. He had spent hours bleeding over the stories, trying to make them new, different.

Already certain passages escaped him, the exact words lost. He knew it would be impossible to recapture the vitality and freshness again. Sure, he could rewrite them. But they'd never be as good.

You're terrific at depressing yourself, Hemingway. Look at the bright side; at least you're on your way out of Lausanne and away from that blasted peace conference. You're going back to Paris. That's something.

Not much.

But something.

There were only three other people in the waiting room—two men and a woman. The men, Slavic-looking characters—one tall and thin, the other squat and hefty—sat along the bench near the door and spoke in muffled, conspiratorial tones. They didn't interest him. But the woman—sitting with her back to him, chain-smoking cigarettes out of a silver holder—was another story.

He hadn't seen her face, but her dark hair was stylishly cut, her coat expensively mink, her pose of indifference damnably challenging. She was flipping through a glossy fashion magazine, apparently oblivious to her plebeian surroundings. Ernest wanted her to turn around so he could see her face.

Guiltily, he thought of Hadley. After they'd made love, she had fallen asleep. He had dressed quietly, leaving the room without waking her. He had left a note, telling her that he expected to be back in two days. He told her not to worry and suggested several places she might enjoy visiting in Lausanne. He loved her more every day, he wrote.

In the hotel lobby, he had telephoned Zack Miles, a reporter for the *Chicago Tribune*. Miles agreed to cover for him while he was in Paris. Miles had heard that a storm near Simplon had delayed the *Express* by an hour.

Now, sitting in the waiting room, his thoughts returned to the damned manuscripts, his mind's eye envisioning the tiny apartment on the rue du Cardinal Lemoine, focusing on the bottom drawer of the desk, the drawer he stuffed with stories and carbons.

They've got to be there. They've got to be.

A porter trod through the waiting room and took up position outside on the platform.

"Train time," Ernest said. He hoped the brunette would turn around. She didn't.

But the two Slavs stared at him strangely. Ernest stared back in his best "fuck you" style. They resumed their conversation. Ernest figured they were talking about farm machinery or some other thrilling subject.

Three minutes later, the *Express* pulled in. He followed the brunette to the fifth car and helped her step aboard. She turned this time, smiling a thank you. She was easily one of the most attractive women he'd ever seen. She was about his age, maybe a year younger. Her heart-shaped face was highlighted by dark green eyes and a full, sensual mouth. Her figure, just visible under her bulky coat, looked exceptional. A conductor opened the door leading to the compartments. "Welcome to the *Orient Express*," he said in a thick, Middle Eastern accent. For Ernest, the conductor's voice conjured up a world of caliphs, seedy marketplaces, and sudden death.

Could be an interesting trip, he thought.

Ernest was wrong about one thing: the two Slavic-looking men in the waiting room were not talking about farm machinery, nor were they farmers.

Waiting near the door, they watched him board, then made sure he stayed on the train. As the *Express* started off, they scurried aboard and settled in the compartment next to his—a location secured through a bribe to the ticket clerk.

"I'm starving," said Strinsky, touching the lobe of his wax ear. The ear had an embarrassing tendency to fall off; hence, Strinsky's habit of touching the waxen earlobe to make sure everything was still in place.

Strinsky's habit annoyed Proskumov. "Stop playing with your damn ear." Proskumov produced a chunk of cheese from his coat.

Strinsky watched distastefully as crumbs of cheese fell on the carpet. He sat opposite Proskumov. "I hope something happens with this Hemingway. I've been bored by this damn peace conference."

"We're just supposed to watch him. See where he goes, make sure he doesn't do anything suspicious." They had been sent to the peace conference to inspect security; once that was accomplished, they'd had little to do.

Until, that is, Beria's cable arrived that afternoon, ordering them to follow Hemingway and regularly file reports with the Cheka agent on duty in the Russian Embassy in Paris.

"Do you know Beria at all?" Proskumov asked, pulling down the window shade.

"Only by reputation."

"I know him. He organized a cell in Baku while I was there. Hard-nosed bastard. A zealot. He loved going underground."

"I thought he was in Tiflis, keeping an eye on the Transcaucasus."

"He was up until a few weeks ago. Then I heard he'd been sent to Paris for something really big."

"You think this Hemingway is involved?"

"Must be—Beria wouldn't be firing off cables and ordering us to follow him if it weren't part of it."

"I still hope Hemingway does something suspicious." Strinsky wanted a chance to impress someone like Beria, someone obviously destined for great things in the party.

"Be patient," said Proskumov. "It's a twelve-hour ride to Paris. Why don't you sit back, relax, and have some cheese."

"I told you—I hate cheese." Strinsky tugged his artificial ear, then tapped his pants pocket, where he kept his knife.

CHAPTER 9

The luxury of the compartment amused Ernest.

Dark brown carpeting—thick enough to sleep on—covered most of the polished parquet floor. Dangling over the settee was a step ladder leading up to a bunk large enough to accommodate two people. At each end of the settee, brass night lamps allowed a passenger to stretch out and read, or look at his toes, or do just about anything he wanted.

A set of towels hung from the side of a small porcelain sink tucked away in a corner. A blue-china water pitcher embossed with the dark blue "WL" logo sat on the adjacent counter. The "WL" stood for Compagnie Internationale des Wagons Lits, the firm that ran the *Express*.

Ernest hung up his coat, then snapped open his overnight case. Settling on the settee, he suppressed a ridiculous urge to giggle; on one of the last train trips he'd made, he'd shared a seat with a Greek farmer and his two fighting cocks. Throughout the trip, the cocks tried to peck and claw each other to death. He'd take the *Orient Express* over the fighting cocks any day.

He read *The Lodger*, the Jack the Ripper novel by Marie Belloc Lowndes. Gertrude Stein had loaned him the book just before he'd left for Lausanne. It was a wonderfully entertaining story. He particularly liked the dark, shadowy, evocative cover. Book covers were important. When his book came out he wanted to have the best cover art he could—

What was he thinking?

When his book came out.

What book?

He didn't even have a manuscript left to show a publisher.

Depressed, he flipped *The Lodger* facedown on the floor. Damn, damn, damn . . .

The *Express* was slowing down. He sat up, glancing out the window. The train was crossing a steel bridge that spanned a small lake. He could see large tables of ice floating in the water. Thick girdered supports were silhouetted against the moon-lit sky. He pressed his face against the cool glass of the window and looked down, watching the ice drift towards the whirlpools which swirled beneath the bridge.

Someone knocked on the door.

"It's open."

An elderly man in a brown uniform—the color of the *chef du train*—leaned into the compartment. *"Billet, s'il vous plaît."*

Ernest handed him his ticket.

"Is the dining car open?" A sudden growl from his stomach had reminded him that he hadn't eaten all day.

"We've kept it open because of the delay—the snowstorm ruined our schedule." The conductor gave Ernest a receipt and padded off towards the next compartment.

Ernest had the dining car to himself, a wonderful opportunity to pretend to be Cornelius Vanderbilt. The waiter, a sleepy-eyed German who shuffled back and forth from the kitchen, apologized for the limited menu. "It's the storm," he said, then served Ernest a wonderful meal of roast duck, potatoes, asparagus, and a delicious red wine. Ernest pretended he knew something of wine when the waiter presented him with the cork for a preliminary sniff. Ernest nodded approval and tried not to think what the meal would cost.

He had just finished when the beautiful woman he'd helped onto the train in Lausanne came into the dining car. Her dark green dress was tight around her generous bosom.

She sat at the table nearest the door. The waiter quickly arrived to take her order, then practically sprinted to the kitchen. Crossing her hands on the table, she stared out the window at the passing darkness.

It was like a scene from a movie, Ernest thought. Here were two people alone in a dining car and neither one acknowledged the other's existence. If it were a movie, it would have to be a comedy. Drama or comedy, she was certainly beautiful enough to be in films.

But, he told himself, he was attracted to her for reasons that went beyond her beauty. She had a mysterious quality—a strange, appealing mixture of arrogance and sadness—that aroused him.

What tripe, he thought. You've had too much wine. Forget her.

But he didn't want to forget her.

He rose and picked up his glass and the bottle of wine. "I hate to eat alone," he said and walked to her table.

She looked past him to the remains of the meal still on his table. "It appears that you already have eaten." Her manner was frosty, her accent German.

He raised the wine bottle. "I also hate to drink alone."

"I'm afraid I'm not drinking tonight."

He was ready to quit. But his interest in her inspired one final salvo. "What about just talking?"

Even her silences were haughty.

"I'm the one who's taking the chance," Ernest said.

"Really?"

"I already know how fascinating I am. But I don't know a damn thing about you. You could turn out to be one of the dullest people on earth."

"Let me assure you that I am."

Ernest started back to his table, then about-faced. "I'm still willing to take my chances."

Finally, she laughed. It wasn't a hearty laugh or a very long one, but it was enough to encourage him to sit down.

"I'm Ernest Hemingway."

"How do you do?" She didn't give her name. Clearly, she wasn't giving anything away.

He filled his glass. "Are you sure you won't join me? I really do hate to drink alone. Makes me feel like an alcoholic."

"In that case, I'll have a little." She stared at him as he poured her half a glass. "Well, Mr. Hemingway—"

"Call me Ernest."

"Well, Mr. Hemingway. What shall we talk about? The weather? Train travel? European politics?"

"Why don't we just swap life stories?"

She sipped her wine. "I'm not sure—"

"I'll go first."

"All right."

"Where should I start?" he asked mockingly. "How's this: I was born on July 21, 1899 in Oak Park, Illinois—"

"We're in trouble already. I'm not divulging my age."

"That's understandable—you must be at least twenty-three."

"No tricks, please. Go on with your biography."

For the next twenty minutes, as she ate dinner, Ernest entertained her with stories that made his life sound as exciting as a novel by Edgar Wallace. It was a narrative only of high points: hunting trips with his father; working the "hospital-mortuary-police station" run for the *Kansas City Star*; enlisting in the Red Cross; driving an ambulance in Italy; getting wounded; coming home a hero; deciding he wanted to be a writer; going to Paris to perfect his skills. The only highlight he left out was Hadley. He blamed the wine for that particular omission.

"What do you write?" she asked, dabbing her lips with a napkin.

"Short stories, mostly. Some poems. And I started a novel but didn't get far. It wasn't any good."

"What are they about?"

He thought for a moment. *What were they about?* It was a question he knew the answer to but didn't like to consider very often; it was better to write than theorize about the actual writing.

"I write about people I know. People I don't. Places I've been too, places I've never seen. Things I've done, things I only imagine."

Christ, Hemingway, you sound like some damn college teacher. Too much vino.

"Spoken like an obscure artist."

"Not obscure. Maybe a little drunk." He refilled her glass, this time to the brim. "Now it's your turn."

"I don't know—"

"You promised."

"I did nothing of the sort. Besides, you're a stranger."

"How can you say that? You know the story of my life."

She slid a cigarette into her holder. Ernest struck a match. "I'm not in the habit of talking to strangers," she said.

"Neither am I."

She laughed. "I don't quite believe you. But maybe strangers are the best people to talk to sometimes." Silver smoke from her cigarette spiraled before her face. "I want to warn you: I can be extremely candid."

"I think I can handle it."

"I grew up in Berlin. My family was—and still is—quite wealthy. Naturally, I went to the best schools, met the best people. One of these best people was my husband. We were married more than a year before I found out about his taste in young men. My family arranged a quiet divorce. I moved to Paris to get away from all that. Several months ago, I met a painter. A Frenchman. I fell in love. At least, I thought I fell in love. We went to Lausanne on holiday. Last night, we had an argument. I realized that I didn't love him at all. He stayed in Lausanne and I took the *Orient Express*, where a brash young American named Hemingway tried to pick me up. End of story."

Ernest feigned outrage. "I assure you my intentions are strictly honorable."

"And I assure you that I don't believe you." She drank the wine, then nudged the glass across the table for a refill. "Are you married?"

"I'm tempted to lie."

"Please don't—you'll disappoint me."

"In that case, yes, I'm married."

"Happily?"

"Usually. But not at the moment."

"What's wrong?"

"Nothing really."

"I thought we were being candid."

Ernest told her about Hadley and the missing manuscripts.

"Is that why you're going back to Paris? To look for them?"

"Actually I'm hoping that the carbon copies are still in the apartment."

"And if they're not?"

"I don't know—maybe try to find the man who stole them."

She brought up her glass. "To your success," she said and finished the wine.

There was nothing left to say. Luckily for Ernest, the waiter had brought separate checks. He tried not to look disturbed as he scanned the waiter's arithmetic.

"Shall we go?" she asked.

Ernest followed her out of the dining car, past the second-class compartments and into the first-class car. She walked down the narrow, carpeted corridor and stopped at the last compartment. He waited for her to ask him in.

She unlocked her door, then reached up and put her hands on his shoulders. "I'm glad we met, Mr. Hemingway. I was feeling sorry for myself before you came over. Now I don't feel at all bad about leaving Lausanne." She kissed him once on the mouth. "Good night."

"You could call me Ernest."

She moved into the darkened compartment. "And I'm Renata Lande. Good night, Ernest." She shut the door.

He stood there, his head throbbing from too much wine, his body shaking from too little sleep. He knuckled the door three times.

"Yes?" she asked through the closed door.

"Why don't we have dinner tomorrow night?"

She didn't answer at first. Ernest listened to the hypnotic clacking of the train wheels on the track. "Where should we meet?" she asked.

"Do you know the Café Deux Magots? It's on the Boulevard St.-Germain."

"Yes, I've been there."

"Eight o'clock?"

"Fine. Good night again, Ernest."

He made his way to the compartment, flipped on the reading lamps, sprawled out on the settee. He was exhausted. Exhausted and more than a little drunk. That was good. He'd fall asleep quickly and not lie awake worrying about the manuscripts and the carbons. He also wouldn't worry about feeling guilty that he had betrayed Hadley by asking Renata Lande out.

He turned on his side in an effort to make himself more comfortable on the settee; he was too tired to climb into the bunk. Through half-closed eyes, he spied the book on the floor.

Damn fine art work, he thought, once again impressed by the shadowy, evocative cover of *The Lodger*.

Fleetingly, he remembered that he had earlier placed the book facedown. Why was it now faceup? Had someone been in the compartment while he was eating?

The questions disturbed him, but only for a few seconds, only until sleep—beautiful, welcome, well-deserved sleep—overtook him for the night.

CHAPTER 10

The plane—a Halberstadt CL 11—was in surprisingly good condition for its age. Although months had passed since Goering's last flight, he piloted the plane superbly; thanks to a generous tailwind, he'd be arriving at the airfield outside Paris ahead of schedule. Early or late, he thought, Kurdorf—stupid, incompetent Kurdorf—had better be there when he landed.

Goering's worst fears were confirmed less than a day earlier when a cable came to party headquarters in Munich. It was from Kurdorf. The Bolsheviks had arranged a deal for the Romanov documents. But something had gone wrong. Kurdorf did not elaborate. Goering had cursed; he had been planning to return by train the following day to Paris and direct the next stage of the operation: to convince the Bolsheviks *and* White Russians that the Nazis had Anastasia, sell her to both factions, then eliminate her—after both sides had paid handsomely.

Now the whole mission was in jeopardy.

In need of speedier transportation, Goering sought out a wealthy friend whose husband owned a plane. He convinced the wife to convince the husband to lend him the aircraft; less than two hours after receiving the cable he took off.

Now, flying over France, Goering tried not to think anymore about Kurdorf—he'd already spent too much of the flight doing that. Flying was one of his few joys. He did not want to sully what little was left of the trip with thoughts of Kurdorf. By his calculations, he had only thirty minutes before landing at Le Bourget airfield.

Behind him the sun peeped through a mass of gray clouds. The sun had always been one of his most reliable allies. He remembered a time when he was flying solo over Bendry, the sun to his back. He observed a single Spad crossing below. He followed the unsuspecting Frenchman for several minutes, virtually invisible in the blinding halo provided by the sun. When the Spad turned, Goering attacked, swooping on the enemy ship, machine guns firing, a line of bullets puncturing the Spad's fuselage. Spewing black smoke, the French plane spiraled to the ground and exploded in a ball of orange flame.

It had been his twenty-second kill of the war. He didn't know it at the time but it was also his last.

How many days had that been before the end of the war? Two? Three? He couldn't say. The memory of his last kill triggered another memory, this one of the last time he met with his men, with the survivors of the most famous fighter squadron in the world. Once commanded by the famed Manfred von Richthofen, the Red Baron, the squad's last leader had been Goering.

He remembered that last night vividly, standing in the middle of the Stiftskeller restaurant near Frankfurt, a glass of *schnapps* in one hand, von Richthofen's walking stick in the other. He proposed a toast to the "glorious history of the first and foremost fighter squadron in Germany."

The armistice was two weeks old. The next day, his men would disperse. The war was over. But Goering would not give up.

"A new battle for the Fatherland has begun. There is much to be proud of, yet much to accomplish. Germany must be rebuilt. The truth is ours and we will prevail. Our time will come again." They drank reverentially, like priests from the chalice, then smashed their glasses against the huge graystone fireplace.

To a man, they felt betrayed by Germany's defeat.

Betrayed. The ensuing years had only increased that sense of betrayal. Germany was collapsing, its leaders unable to lead, its people lost and despairing. That was why Goering admired Hitler. Hitler had ideas, plans. He could command. People listened to him, responded to him. Germany needed Hitler. And so did Goering.

Ahead to the west, Goering could make out the faint outline of the Eiffel Tower. Banking left, he dropped two hundred feet. A small town—Epernay, if his map was right—disappeared under his wings. The airfield was only a few kilometers away. He sipped from the brandy flask he always packed when he flew.

He checked his watch. Ten A.M. Even with two refueling stops, the last in Strasbourg where he took five minutes to drink three cups of coffee and eat several pastries, he had made excellent time.

Le Bourget came into view: four tin hangars and half-a-dozen or so crisscrossing runways. Goering saw a black limousine—perhaps the Mercedes—parked near the farthest hangar. He banked over the hangar, dipping close enough to see Kurdorf standing next to the limousine. Then he turned, made his approach and jostled along the pitted runway. The propeller hurled streaks of mud into the air. He taxied toward the far hangar.

As he switched off the engine, Kurdorf appeared. Ignoring Kurdorf's helping hand, Goering climbed out of the plane. He removed his dirt-caked goggles and wiped his face with a handkerchief. Kurdorf seemed nervous, frightened. As well he should. Goering had nothing but contempt for Kurdorf.

"Did you arrange for fuel and a place to keep the plane?" Goering asked.

"It's all taken care of."

"Who's in the car?"

"Dietrich."

Pulling up the collar of his coat, Goering motioned to the hangar. "Let's go in there."

As soon as they entered the deserted hangar, Goering slapped Kurdorf twice across the face, hard slaps that cut Kurdorf's lip and drew blood.

"Fool!" Goering said.

Tears welled in Kurdorf's eyes. He dabbed at his lip with his hand. "I don't need to be struck."

"You don't? Our entire operation is in jeopardy because of you."

"I did everything I could. You should have been here."

Goering pushed Kurdorf against a row of abandoned lockers. "I don't answer to you—you answer to me. And I want to know what went wrong. Now."

Kurdorf sat on a low wooden bench in front of the lockers. The hangar smelled sickeningly of oil. Staring at the concrete floor, Kurdorf related his first meeting with Beria and the plan to exchange the Romanov documents at the Gare de

Lyon. When he got to the part where Beria had demanded that their courier come alone, Goering interrupted.

"You went along with that?"

Kurdorf mumbled a reply. The oil smell was making him sick.

"I didn't hear you," said Goering.

"I said that I thought it wise to do what he said."

Goering turned his back on Kurdorf. "You really are a fool."

Kurdorf thought it best not to respond.

"Did Schmidt return?"

"No."

"And the Bolsheviks? Have you heard from them?"

"Beria contacted us last night. We met at the same place. He was furious. He said that his man waited for hours and our courier never showed up. When the Bolshevik waiting in the station saw a bag he thought might be the right one, he stole it."

"And?"

"It was nothing. Beria gave the bag to us. It's filled with a lot of nonsense, writing by some American journalist."

"A journalist! What's his name?"

"Hemingway. Ernest Hemingway. The valise is in the car. Beria said they searched the man's apartment but found nothing suspicious."

"Don't be stupid enough to believe Beria. For all we know, Beria's men did away with Schmidt and took the documents. Where does this American live?"

"Somewhere on the Left Bank. His address is on one of the papers in the bag." Kurdorf was confused. What possible importance was Hemingway? His involvement was all a mistake. "Why are you interested in Hemingway?"

Goering ignored Kurdorf. He paced the length of the hangar, then returned to Kurdorf. "I hope for your sake that you followed my orders and kept half the Romanov documents."

"I did exactly what you told me." Kurdorf refrained from asking Goering why half the documents were held back. Goering headed out of the hangar. Kurdorf followed. Across the field, a man tried to coax two swaybacked horses to pull an overturned plane from the mud. It started to rain.

"Where are we going?" asked Kurdorf.

"To Hemingway's apartment." They reached the Mercedes.

"Why?"

"Because he might have some answers. I'm not taking Beria's word for it."

"But Beria said that Hemingway was in Lausanne."

"You really are a moron, aren't you? Beria is not our ally. Only believe what you see with your own eyes. Perhaps Hemingway has returned since yesterday. I'd be interested to talk to him. He may not be as innocent as your friend Beria would have you believe."

"Beria is not my friend."

"Of course not."

Kurdorf sat in the back seat of the Mercedes, wishing suddenly that he was back in Munich, living with his sister and working as a bookkeeper. He stared forlornly out the window.

CHAPTER 11

Despite a hangover, Ernest was first off when the *Express* pulled into the Gare de Lyon shortly before eleven. Running along the platform, he looked about for Renata but didn't see her.

At the stationmaster's office, a fossilized clerk told him that no one had turned in a valise matching the description of the stolen case. Ernest wasn't surprised.

He left the station and jogged along the Seine. The crisp, cold air relieved much of his hangover and soon he was running along the quai at a brisk pace. Fishermen, their long cane poles tucked under their arms as they warmed their hands in their pockets, shook their heads as he passed; fishing the river in the freezing cold made perfect sense to them. Running along the Seine was just crazy.

Ernest crossed the Pont Sully and started up the hill to the rue du Cardinal Lemoine, a narrow, cobblestone street in the working-class part of the Latin Quarter. Ernest's building was number 74, a whitewashed, four-story affair next to a dance hall.

Opening the door on the ground floor, the familiar scent of onions stung his senses. Madame Rivette, the concierge, seemed to subsist totally on onions. Holding his breath against the odor, he took the steps three at a time up the spiral staircase to the fourth-floor apartment.

He had the key in the lock before he realized that the door was ajar. Cautiously, he entered.

The place was a shambles. Clothes thrown on the floor, chairs overturned, dishes smashed. In the bedroom, the mattress on the huge bed had been pushed off and slit. As Ernest angrily shoved the mattress back onto the bed, feathers glided through the air like snowflakes.

"Jesus Christ!" he said, surveying the damage. "Jesus H. fucking Christ!"

A mixture of confusion and outrage filled him. Confusion: Who was behind this? Were they the same bastards who had stolen his manuscripts? Why had they done it? Outrage: He felt violated. Someone had broken into his apartment. Someone had taken what was his. And he had no one to lash out at. Had he found anyone in the apartment, he knew he would have killed him.

On the floor in the living room he found the original manuscript to *Up in Michigan*, one of his stories. Gertrude Stein said it was good but unpublishable—its sexual content too strong. He remembered that he'd kept that story apart from the others, planning to reread it. Hadley must have overlooked it when she had packed the rest of the stuff.

At least one story is left, he thought bitterly. The one nobody will publish. You're riding one hell of a lucky streak, Hemingway.

Angrily, he picked up a porcelain shaving cup Hadley had given him and smashed it against the wall.

He then quickly went through the rest of the apartment. Nothing. No stories. No poems. And worst of all, no carbons. He hastened down the stairs to the concierge's apartment. No one was there.

Back in his own apartment, he poured himself a glass of Hadley's sherry. He hated sherry but it was the only alcohol in the house. After one drink, he abandoned the glass in favor of the whole bottle and settled on the windowsill overlooking the rue du Cardinal Lemoine.

What the hell is going on? he asked himself, trying to figure out why anyone would steal his manuscripts and ransack his apartment. It made no sense; he knew from the number of rejection slips that his manuscripts were of no value to anyone but him. And he and Hadley had no jewels, no rare paintings. What was it all about?

Damned if I know, he thought as he finished the sherry. He considered going to the police. The police would listen but what could they do? He had no proof there was any connection between the stolen manuscripts and the ransacked apartment. He had no suspects. He would be wasting his time as well as the police's.

With the sherry gone, he debated whether to walk to

Montparnasse and get drunk at the Rotonde or Select. But he wasn't wild about either place. Only last month, he'd gotten into a fight at the Rotonde with a particularly obnoxious artist named Mangini. Three waiters had had to pull them apart. The problem with the Rotonde and Select was that they were filled with Manginis, all obsessed with themselves and their so-called art.

He looked out the window. The man who owned the dance hall was sweeping garbage into the gutter. Crossing the street was a man dressed in black carrying a long wooden box and several brooms—a chimney sweep. Ernest watched the sweep disappear around the corner.

The bottle dropped from Ernest's hand, shattering on the floor. Goddamn it! Wasn't anything going right? He was about to pick up the pieces when he noticed a car edge down the street and stop in front of his building. The car was dark and badly scarred. Ernest thought it was a Mercedes.

A man got out of the car and approached Duviver, the dance hall owner. Ernest guessed the man was asking directions. Paris was a city of lost tourists. Duviver nodded his head and the stranger motioned to the Mercedes. Two more men emerged from the car, the taller one wearing a leather coat, the kind German pilots favored during the war. All three men surrounded Duviver. Duviver nodded some more, then suddenly looked up, pointing towards Ernest's apartment. The eyes of the strangers followed Duviver's arm.

Christ, thought Ernest, they're looking for me! Instinctively, he backed away from the window. Seconds passed. He chanced a look out the window. Duviver had resumed sweeping. The men were gone. The Mercedes was still there, empty.

Ernest pushed through the door and peered down the stairwell. The men were on the second floor, tearing up the stairs.

Ernest ran to the top floor. A wooden ladder led to the roof. As he climbed up the ladder, he heard the men barge into his apartment.

He snapped two small metal locks and tried to shoulder open the trapdoor to the roof. It wouldn't give. He heard footsteps on the stairs below him. He pushed against the trapdoor. A hand wrapped around his left ankle. The trapdoor opened. Ernest kicked down hard with his right foot, pounding against what felt like an arm. He didn't look down.

He kicked again and felt the hand slip off. He pulled himself up and onto the roof.

Ernest hid behind a chimney to the right of the trapdoor. Someone was climbing up. He waited, ticking off five seconds in his mind.

One. A pigeon glided onto the rooftop.

Two. A page of a newspaper blew in the wind.

Three. He balled his right hand into a tight fist.

Four. The pigeon flew away.

Five. Ernest sprang out. The man was just bringing his right leg onto the roof. He was young and clean shaven. Ernest hit him in the face. Blood spurted from the man's nose. His eyes lit up with surprise. Ernest hit him again and he fell down the ladder.

Ernest jumped down ten feet to the top of the adjacent building. The next two buildings were each three stories high. Ernest could see the dome of the Panthéon several blocks away. The next building was higher. Ernest clambered up the slanted roof, pausing at the top to look behind.

A man with a gun stood near the trapdoor on his building. Ernest rolled across the roof and scurried behind another chimney. Peeking around the chimney's corner he realized it was the man he had hit. Another man appeared. Together they started toward Ernest.

Ernest ran across two more buildings and then stopped. An alleyway, at least twelve feet wide, separated him from the next building. Five stories below, children played a game of hide and seek in the alley.

Ernest didn't want to jump across. The broad jump had never been his sport. In fact, he'd never really been that good at football because of his feet, over which he had a habit of tripping. He didn't feel like tripping and falling fifty feet to his death.

There was a sudden cracking sound and a piece of the roof blew off near his feet. Five buildings away stood the two men, the one with the gun taking aim. Ernest zigzagged back several feet. He heard another shot, felt nothing. Then he ran, pushing off the roof with all his strength.

He almost made it.

With his legs kicking, his arms flailing, he hit the top of the side of the opposite building, just managing to get his arms over the low ledge that ran along the length of the roof. The collision nearly knocked him out. Below, the children played their game, oblivious to his plight. Feeling his left arm about to break, he let go. He dangled from the roof by only one hand.

He clawed at the brick wall with his left hand, trying to get another grip. His fingernails scraped against the brick. He turned his head to the left. His pursuers were leaping onto a roof just four buildings away.

Then his right hand started to slip.

"Goddamn it!" he shouted. Below, a young girl had looked up and begun to scream. Ernest lost his grip. He fell.

A hand—the blackest hand Ernest had ever seen—reached down and clutched at his arm. Another black hand followed and pulled him up.

Ernest fell against his savior and together they tumbled onto the roof. A dark puff of smoke rose from the man, whose face was as black as his hands. He wore a black coat. A hair net covered his head. Ernest had been saved by the chimney sweep.

"Christ, thanks. If ever I needed a helping hand it was then."

"You should try walking instead of flying—it's safer."

"I'll remember that." He stood up. The soot from the sweep had rubbed into his clothes. Ernest helped the man up.

Across the alley stood the two men. They were not about to risk the jump. The man kept his gun by his side. Ernest understood then that the two previous shots had been meant to scare him, not kill him. Arrogantly, he gave the men the finger, the way he'd seen an Italian reporter do to Mussolini in Lausanne. The men turned around, looking for a way to the street.

"Do all these buildings have stairs to the roof?"

"Some do, some don't. The one your friends are on does not."

"What about this one?"

"*Oui*." The sweep led Ernest to a trapdoor set near a drain pipe.

"Thank you, my friend," said Ernest shaking the sweep's hand.

The man smiled. His teeth shone like a minstrel performer's. "People usually don't like to shake my hand while I'm working."

"Anytime, my friend, anytime. Come to the Amateurs some night and let me buy you a drink."

"I will."

"Thanks again. I owe you. But I'm afraid I can't stick around to chat."

Ernest looked across the alleyway. The two men were moving back toward his building, stopping along each roof to check for an exit to the street.

Ernest gave the sweep a friendly slap on the back and then climbed down the ladder. At the foot of the ladder, he found himself on a cramped landing. He descended the stairs calmly, even saying hello to the old man who was cleaning out the *pissoir*.

When Ernest came out of the building, he took a moment to pinpoint his location; the chase along the rooftops had turned him around.

Dozens of bums—*clochards*—were sitting on the ground, mumbling to themselves, some pressing bottles of cheap wine to their lips. Ernest then knew where he was—in the Rue Contrescarpe, a block away from his apartment.

Turning right, he headed down the Rue Mouffetard, stopping several times to browse at the fruit and vegetable stands that lined the street. Each time, he made sure to look behind to see if someone were following. No one was.

His legs hurt and his hands were badly scraped. Other than that, he was unharmed, at least physically. But he knew enough from the war to know that soon the impact of what had just happened—the idea that he had come close to getting killed—would hit him.

He needed a drink and he didn't care much where he got it. There was a cafe on the Boulevard Saint-Marcel that was a good place to go to be left alone. He wanted to be alone. He needed time to get some thinking done, try to figure out what was going on or, more realistically, try to figure out how he could go about finding out what was going on.

A crowd had gathered outside Saint-Medard's Church to watch a fire-eater ply his trade. The man, naked to the waist, took a mouthful of gasoline, then asked for volunteers to light a match for him. Ernest walked on; he'd seen the show before.

He waited at the corner for traffic to clear. Something pressed into the small of his back.

"Just pretend we're old friends," whispered a man in a thick German accent.

"Why should I?"

The pressure moved from Ernest's back to his left side as the man took a step forward. It was the third man from the Mercedes, the one with the pilot's coat. "It's very simple. This is a gun—a gun I won't hesitate to use. Believe me."

Ernest believed him.

CHAPTER 12

The Mercedes was parked a block from the Boulevard Saint-Marcel. Behind the steering wheel sat the clean-shaven character Ernest had belted down the ladder. He looked about twenty-seven or twenty-eight, not as young as Ernest had first thought. Pressing a blood-soaked handkerchief to his nose, he glared as Ernest gingerly settled in the back seat.

The middle-aged man next to the driver squinted through thick-lensed glasses. He breathed heavily from his exertions across the rooftops. He studied Ernest warily, then looked away.

Ernest turned his attention to the man with the gun. About thirty, he figured, probably a former officer, judging from the coat. The man's searing blue eyes boldly returned Ernest's gaze.

"Turn to the left," the man told Ernest.

"Fuck you."

The man raised the gun, a Colt .45 automatic. One shot at this range would send the better part of Ernest's head onto the street. He did as he was told.

He was blindfolded and his hands were tied firmly behind his back. He leaned forward, twisting his wrists to keep his blood moving in his hands. The car pulled away from the curb.

Ernest tried to follow their route in his mind, envisioning a Paris street map. He gave up after ten minutes. By his calculations, they were either near the Eiffel Tower or Notre-Dame, two sites far enough apart to suggest that in all probability they had been driving in circles, undoubtedly to confuse him. It had worked—he knew wherever they were it was nowhere near those two landmarks.

"How about letting me know where we're going?"

"Keep quiet."

"It's just that I have a dinner date tonight that I don't want to—"

The butt of the .45 smashed against Ernest's right knee. The pain was excruciating. Ernest held back a scream. He wouldn't give these bastards any satisfaction. Biting hard into his lower lip, he thought about a certain lake in Michigan; Hadley on their wedding day; the Forbes and Forsetti gym in Chicago—anything to divert his mind from the pain.

"As I said—keep quiet."

"All right."

Sweat rolled off Ernest's forehead. He wanted to piss in the worst way. And he was scared.

He didn't mind being frightened. He'd fought with his share of fear during the war and he'd come out of that okay. Fear was natural. Without fear, you couldn't have courage.

The trick was how you acted when you were scared.

He took several deep breaths. He was reacting, in part, to his near fatal fall from the building. He wished he'd had the chance to get a drink.

He said nothing, fairly certain that they weren't going to kill him, at least not right away. When they could have killed him—once on the roof, and once as he waited for the traffic to pass—they didn't. Clearly, they wanted to talk to him. What they wanted to discuss baffled him.

The car slowed and stopped. The doors banged open. Someone eased him out of the back seat. He sensed that his guide was the little man with the myopic glasses.

To keep the characters straight in his mind, he dubbed the little man Glasses, the man he'd smacked on the roof Nose, and the man in the fancy coat—who was obviously their leader—The Pilot.

The sweet, sickening smell of rancid garbage filled the air outside the car. A wooden door creaked open. He was led past the door. A voice he'd never heard before said: "We're going down some stairs. Be careful."

Ernest nodded. He took the first step, then stumbled. "Sorry," he said, taking his time before starting again down the steps.

A door opened above him and he heard female laughter. The smell of cigarettes and perfume replaced the odor of garbage that had drifted in. Someone spoke in German and the door was closed. Silence replaced the laughter. The perfume lingered.

The metal stairway was narrow and winding. Ernest tripped three times. He counted eighty-seven steps before they reached a dirt-covered floor. The air was musty. Ernest felt two men brush past him.

Glasses—Ernest was sure this was his guide—sneezed as dust filled the air.

"*Gesundheit*," Ernest said.

The man started to say "*Danke*" but then thought better of it. He pushed Ernest, as if to tell him that even the most innocent conversation was forbidden.

Ernest counted one hundred and twenty paces before Glasses turned him to the left. They walked a few more feet, then stopped. Nose and The Pilot went on ahead. Ernest heard several men speaking German. He'd taught himself a little German—but not enough to help him translate.

The three minutes that passed felt like an eternity to Ernest. It was the blindfold. There was something about not being able to see, something that made you feel totally helpless. It was a feeling he didn't like.

Glasses led him forward, then shoved him through a doorway. His blindfold was removed. His hands remained tied.

"Sit down, Hemingway." The Pilot indicated a high-backed wooden chair in the middle of the room.

Ernest didn't budge.

Glasses came into the room. Nose stood in the doorway, a carbine resting across his arms. The room was dark, lit by a single torch flickering from one wall. The walls were rock, rough-hewn, and jagged. The chair was the sole piece of furniture.

"Sit down."

"I'd rather stand if it's all the same to you."

The Pilot smiled, his right hand waving his gun. "I can empty the clip and no one but us will hear the shots. Sit down."

"My legs are kind of tired," Ernest said, plunking down on the uncomfortable chair.

His smile vanishing, The Pilot circled Ernest, tapping the butt of the pistol against the palm of his hand. Glasses stood in the corner, trying to disappear in the shadows. Ernest crossed his legs, hoping to appear calm.

"What is your full name?" The Pilot asked.

"Ernest Miller Hemingway."

"Nationality?"

"American. And I bet you guys are German."

The Pilot stopped directly in front of Ernest. "Your sense of humor leaves me unamused. Save your jokes for your infantile countrymen."

Ernest wanted to tell him to go to hell, but the odds weren't in it. He nodded and uncrossed his legs, uncomfortable with such subservience. He worked his hands against the ropes.

"What are you doing in Paris?"

"I like onion soup."

The Pilot chuckled. For a moment, Ernest thought that he was going to get away with the wisecrack. But then The Pilot slashed the butt of the .45 across Ernest's face. Ernest fell to the floor. His face hurt like hell but nothing was broken and he knew that The Pilot had deliberately held back. He pulled himself onto the chair.

"I'm a writer—I came to Paris to write."

"What do you write?"

"Lots of things."

The Pilot resumed circling. "We're all educated men. Tell us exactly what you write."

"Short stories. Some poetry."

"Have you been published?"

"Just once."

"So you're a struggling writer."

"Is there any other kind?"

"But you also write for newspapers."

How the hell did he know that? "When I need the money."

"Were you working as a journalist in Lausanne?"

That surprised Ernest. Then he realized that several people in their building, including the gossipy Madame Rivette, knew he'd gone to Lausanne. Anyone of them could have told the Krauts.

"Yeah—I was there as a reporter."

The Pilot stopped behind Ernest. "In case you're wondering, a man named Burchardt told me. Nicholas Burchardt."

"I don't know any Burchardt. Never have. Maybe you

picked up the wrong Hemingway, Fritz." Ernest fully expected another encounter with the .45. He was too angry to really care.

"Your attempts to provoke are juvenile."

Ernest peered at Glasses in the shadows. Glasses moved back as far as possible, as if Ernest's look could somehow harm him.

"Perhaps it wasn't Burchardt. It could have been a Russian named Beria."

"Never heard of Beria. Can I go now?"

The Pilot walked in front of Ernest. "When did you come back to Paris from Lausanne?"

"This morning. I had a hell of a homecoming. You bastards didn't happen to ransack my apartment?"

"Why did you come back?"

Ernest was tired of the interrogation. He had hoped to learn something—anything—about his manuscripts. So far, all he had was two names—Burchardt and Beria. And he was sure that The Pilot was too smart to give anything important away for free.

"Listen, Fritz, I'm getting a little sick and tired of this. First we go for a stroll across the roofs of the Latin Quarter—different and invigorating and a little dangerous. Next is the blindfold act as we drive to these lovely surroundings. Who's your landlord? The Phantom of the Opera? Why don't you tell me something for a change."

"Do all American writers talk so much? No matter—I know why you returned to Paris. You wanted to look for your missing manuscripts."

That perked Ernest up. "What do you know about them?"

"Quite a bit. In fact, I happen to have them. I even read one of your stories, something about a journalist in Kansas City. I thought Kansas City was a place with cowboys."

"Why did you take the manuscripts?"

Glasses suddenly launched into a coughing fit so severe that he fled the chamber. The Pilot smirked at his departure. "We didn't take them. Someone else did. We . . . inherited them."

"I want them back."

"Of course. Just as we want our own documents returned."

Our documents. Here, at last, was a clue, thought Ernest. The documents, whatever the hell they were, had something to do with his kidnapping, something to do with the theft of his manuscripts. Something, but what?

"What documents?" asked Ernest.

"Does the dialogue in your stories ring as false as that? If so, I advise you to consider another career."

"The only document I have is my passport. What documents are you talking about?"

"The Romanov papers."

Romanov papers? What had he to do with the murdered royal family of Russia, assuming those were the Romanovs the German meant? Was it that story he'd written about the White Russians in Paris? Every waiter and bellboy with a Russian accent claimed to be a nobleman forced to flee the Bolshevik hordes. All waxed poetic over the Czar and Czarina. Some even cried on cue and claimed to be related to the Czar.

That story was the closest he'd come to the Romanovs.

"I've never seen any Romanov papers," said Ernest. "I don't know what the hell you're talking about."

Glasses edged into the room. Pilot pocketed his .45. "I believe you," he said.

"I want my stories back."

The Pilot walked over to Glasses and spoke quietly. Then he called Nose into the room.

Only Glasses faced Ernest, and his eyes were fixed on The Pilot's face.

Ernest stood and stormed across the room, barreling into the huddle. Everyone went down. Ernest scurried up and made it out the door. He stopped dead. A fourth man, also shouldering a rifle, was stationed in a dark corridor.

Ernest smiled as the guard lowered his rifle level with Ernest's chest. Ernest looked down the narrow, dusty corridor, trying to gauge where the hell he was. But it was too dark.

The other three Germans emerged from the room. Dusting off his coat, The Pilot approached Ernest.

"I want those manuscripts back," Ernest said.

The Pilot backhanded him across the face, splitting Ernest's lower lip. "Take him out and kill him," said The Pilot as he started down the corridor and vanished in the darkness.

Ernest couldn't believe what he'd just heard. He didn't mind dying for a decent cause but so far no one had bothered to tell him why he was about to become a martyr. "Listen, if you want the stories that bad you can have them. Just save me the carbon copies."

Glasses reached up and secured the blindfold over Ernest's eyes.

"That was a joke," Ernest said.

But nobody—not even Ernest—was laughing.

They drove for ten minutes before Ernest spoke. "Since you guys have the guns, do we really need the blindfold?"

Ernest didn't expect anything to happen. But then—to his amazement—the blindfold was untied and he could see: first, Glasses sitting next to him in the back of the Mercedes, pistol clutched firmly in his right mitt; then Nose, braking the car for a red light.

A sheepish sun peeked through the clouds and gilded the bare treetops along the Boulevard Raspail. Old women dressed in black lugged grocery-filled canvas bags up the hill; two artists, their paint-splattered smocks paltry defense against the cold, stood on the corner of the rue Daguerre and shook hands. A whore propositioned them. They waved her away.

Ernest debated whether to yell for help, then decided against it. For one thing, Glasses was a scared man, the kind who probably had never used a gun before and therefore was most likely to shoot at the smallest provocation. And Ernest just wasn't the sort who went around yelling. It wasn't his style.

The light turned green and Nose steered the Mercedes through the traffic. They didn't seem to be in a great hurry.

"Ever kill a man before?" asked Ernest.

Glasses looked away. "We can always put the blindfold around your mouth."

"What's wrong with a little conversation? Consider it my last request—isn't that what a condemned man usually gets?"

"Talk about something else."

Nose turned onto the Boulevard Montparnasse. Customers crowded the Café Dome on the corner.

"Okay, let's see . . . where you boys from? Berlin? Munich? I never met a German who wasn't from one of those burgs."

Glasses edged back in his seat.

"I bet it's Berlin," said Ernest. "Ever been to the Vokoban Cafe?"

They turned onto the Boulevard St.-Michel. Glasses stared out the window, watching the Luxembourg Gardens come into view.

"You must have been there," Ernest said.

Glasses sighed. "Yes. Many times."

Glasses was a lousy liar. There was no Vokoban Café. Ernest had made it up. That meant they were probably from Munich. "Germany's a beautiful country. Great people. The war was a terrible tragedy." Glasses had put Ernest in the mood to lie.

"Yes, it was."

"Were you in it?"

Glasses didn't answer.

"I was—drove an ambulance for the Red Cross."

Nose snickered.

"What's the matter, Hans? Got something against the RC?"

"Don't call me Hans."

"Sure. What's your handle? Seigfried? Wilhelm? Friedrich?" Ernest wanted Nose mad, mad enough to make a mistake.

Another red light, this time at the rue Soufflot. Ernest hated red lights; he remembered cursing the day the Paris city fathers had installed the signals. But today he thought that red lights were the most wonderful idea in the world. Anything was that gave him a few minutes to think of a way to save his life.

The light changed green four cars ahead but traffic didn't move. Irate drivers punched their horns. The front car spurted through the intersection just as green turned to red.

Glasses asked Nose something in German. Nose shrugged.

The cause of the delay came into view. A man with a painted white face—a mime—was doing little routines, hoping to snare some loose francs from generous motorists.

Ernest hated mimes almost as much as he hated red lights. Mimes were far too precious for his taste. But at this particular moment, the mime was a godsend, at least if he got to the car before the light turned.

Working his wrists back and forth, Ernest watched the mime palm some money from the driver of the first car. The mime passed the second car—the driver was shaking his head—and then stopped next to the car directly ahead.

Damn it! There wasn't enough time. The light was sure to change. Blood trickled down Ernest's hands as he snapped his wrists against the rope.

The mime pretended he was a bullfighter, executing a stirring *veronica* as an imaginary bull brushed past. Ernest had never seen a bullfight but the pantomime was convincing. The driver of the car obviously thought so too, for he was fishing through his pockets for change.

Ernest stared at the light, expecting it to switch to green at any moment.

Ernest slipped his left hand out of the rope. He kept both hands behind his back. Glasses was watching the mime accept his money.

The light changed.

Nose hit the horn impatiently.

The mime approached the Mercedes. Nose shook his head. Ernest nodded his.

Traffic moved.

The mime pressed his face against the side window, leaving a fine dusting of white makeup on the glass. Concerned that the mime might spot the gun, Glasses swept the .45 under the flap of his coat.

Ernest made his move.

Pushing Glasses with his right hand, Ernest pulled up the handle, shoved open the door and jumped, tumbling with the mime along the street.

"For Christ's sake!" the mime said uncharacteristically.

Nose braked the Mercedes. Tires screeched. Horns blared.

Ernest picked himself up and ran, ran down the rue de Vaugirard, past the astonished eyes of yet more old ladies in black; ran, ran into the Luxembourg Gardens, past the ice-covered fountain, past an elderly man tossing bread crumbs into a flock of pigeons, past the bust of Flaubert. He came out of the gardens and sprinted down the rue de Fleurus. He went into the courtyard of a whitewashed building on the left, where, out of breath, gasping, he pounded on the door, waiting for someone to open up, wondering where he'd go if no one was home.

* * *

Kurdorf would have lost Hemingway if it hadn't been for Goering's foresight. Goering had ordered one of the men, a fellow named Hessler, to follow the Mercedes on a bicycle. This Hessler had done. So when Hemingway bolted, Hessler had tailed him, then gone back for Kurdorf, who was puffing through the Luxembourg Gardens.

Kurdorf listened to Hessler, then went to a nearby call box. Goering picked up on the first ring. "Did he get away?"

"Yes."

"Did he suspect?"

"No—it worked out nicely."

"Good. Where is he now?"

"He went into an apartment at 27, rue de Fleurus."

"That means nothing to me. Any idea who lives there?"

"None at all."

"Try to find out. But stay with him. That's most important."

"I will."

"And Kurdorf—"

"Yes?"

"Good work." Goering hung up.

CHAPTER 13

"Come in and sit down," Gertrude Stein said. "You look all disheveled."

Smiling a thank you to the maid who had let him in, Ernest stood for a moment just outside Miss Stein's study. He always hesitated before entering the room, always let his eyes scan the walls, drinking in the Picassos, Cézannes, Matisses. This was his homage to Miss Stein, a small ritual he felt made her happy. And Ernest most definitely wanted to make Miss Stein happy; there was much she could teach him about writing, much she could do to advance his career.

She sat in a big, overstuffed chair directly beneath the stark, bold portrait Picasso had done of her. She was a large woman and Picasso had painted her just that way, posing her aggressively with her body arched forward, one hand splayed on her knee. She seemed ready to get up and leave, impatient to get to her own work. Picasso had perfectly caught her face: the long nose, broad mouth, dark probing eyes, short bundled hair.

Just a few wrinkles betrayed the sixteen years since Picasso had painted the portrait. The years had done nothing to dull her aggressiveness.

"Sit here," she said, gesturing to an ottoman that only seconds before had held her feet. "Have some raspberry liqueur. And tell me all."

While Ernest really wanted a double whiskey, homemade liqueur was a Stein speciality and he didn't want to offend. He took the glass and sipped; the liqueur spread welcome warmth through his chilled body.

"Tastes good," he said. "Where's Alice?" He didn't much like Alice Toklas. And he sensed that she didn't like him much, either. But he made a point of always acting courteously toward her.

"Forget the small talk and explain your sordid appearance. Have you been boxing again?"

"Not exactly." Ernest's lip hurt when he spoke. "It's a long, long story."

"In that case, edit it to a short, short story. You can use the practice." She looked beyond Ernest. "Ah," she said. "Alice arrives just in time."

Ernest rose as Toklas padded into the room. She was a dark, sad-faced woman with a beakish nose and close-cropped hair. "Hello, Ernest," she said pleasantly, taking a chair to Stein's left.

"Ernest was about to launch into a story."

"Wonderful—I love Ernest's stories." Her tone told Ernest that she didn't like his stories at all. Toklas disliked him, he thought, because Stein was so fond of him.

The maid served tea and tiny cakes. Ravenous, Ernest popped three cakes into his mouth.

"For God's sakes, Hemingway, eat later and get on with your tale. Never keep an audience waiting too long."

Ernest told his story the way he would have written it, with few descriptions and almost no adverbs and adjectives. He started with the theft of the manuscripts, moved to the ransacked apartment, then to the chase across the rooftops, glossing over his rather flat-footed jump. Relating the kidnapping, he expertly mimicked his captors' German accents. Even Toklas smiled. When he finished, he was nearly as breathless as when he'd first come in.

"Wonderful!" said Stein, clapping. "Now how much of it is true?"

Ernest was shocked. He hadn't considered that anyone would doubt him. "It's all true. Every word."

Toklas leaned over the fireplace, adding more logs and stoking the fire. "I believe you."

"I'm glad somebody around here does."

"Don't be offended," Stein said. "I was just teasing. Really, Hemingway, your gloominess surprises me. I've never seen you like this before."

"I've never been kidnapped before. It's not the kind of thing that makes your day."

"I thought you liked adventure," Toklas said.

"When it makes sense. When I have at least a vague idea as to what it's all about."

The fire sputtered and cackled. An ash shot into the air and landed on Stein's slipper. Toklas reached down and patted the slipper, smothering the ash.

"Let's take the story apart bit by bit," said Stein, handing Ernest a pad and pencil. "You make notes—I was up all night writing and my fingers ache."

Ernest was beginning to regret coming here. While Miss Stein was a hell of a writing teacher, he didn't place much faith in her abilities as a detective.

"Number one," she announced dramatically. "We know the Germans have your manuscripts. They say someone else stole them from the Gare de Lyon. Why would anyone do that?"

Ernest chuckled. "I've been trying to figure that one out for the last day."

"Perhaps they're lovers of literature," said Toklas.

Stein looked at her sourly. "Don't be silly."

Ernest doodled.

"Are you taking all this down?"

"Every word."

"Good. Now, the Germans suspected that you had these 'Romanov documents,' whatever they may be. You don't have them, do you?"

"Never heard of them."

Shivering, Toklas crossed her arms. "Do you think these documents have anything to do with the Czar?"

"The late Czar," Stein observed.

"I have no idea. It's possible. But it could also be a code name or something. I just don't know."

"All right . . . good . . . let me think." Stein stroked her chin. "These Germans brought you somewhere underground, you said. A cavern of some sort."

"Yeah. It smelled like a cave and it was dark, very dark."

"And in Paris?"

"Absolutely."

"Sounds very Dante-esque," Toklas said. "Perhaps it was the eighth circle of hell."

"You're not being very constructive," snapped Stein. "Ernest came here for help—not sarcasm."

Toklas looked sadly into the fireplace, pained by the rebuke. Ernest suppressed a vindictive smile.

"I don't know of any underground caverns in Paris," said Stein.

"Neither do I."

"Well, that doesn't help us very much." Pause: Ernest finished off the pastry and admired the paintings on the opposite wall.

Stein broke the silence. "The Germans are the key."

No shit! thought Ernest.

"In that case," said Toklas, striving to make amends, "Ernest should go see Louis Offenbach."

"Offenbach! Of course," said Stein as if she'd just solved the mystery. "Ernest should go see Offenbach."

"Offenbach is a prick." Ernest meant it—Offenbach *was* a prick—but he also delighted in offending Toklas's rather prim sensibilities.

"No doubt he has one," Stein said. "I don't know him well enough to know if he is one."

"Take my word for it."

"What if he is?" asked Toklas. "Louis Offenbach knows everything there is to know about the German community in Paris."

"Alice is right. A German can't pass wind around here without Offenbach knowing about it."

Ernest couldn't resist. "That's because he's got his nose up every Kraut asshole in Paris."

"I wish we could save the earthiness for Ernest's short stories," sniffed Toklas.

"Offenbach is not one of my favorites," said Ernest. "And I'm not one of his."

"Don't tell me you beat him up!"

Stein laughed. "Alice is under the impression that at one time or another you have placed your meaty fist against the jaw of nearly every male in Europe."

Ernest glanced at Toklas, thinking half-seriously that there was at least one female in Europe he'd like to place his "meaty" fist against. "As a matter of fact," he said, "I did belt him once. I was having a drink at Harry's and he came up to me and said that he'd heard a rumor that all those stories about me getting shot up and saving a guy's life in the war were all fiction. So I pulled up my pants and showed him the scars. Then I hit him."

"That changes nothing," Stein said. "He's still the man to see. I admit there is an unsavory side to him. He once published a particularly vicious lie about Picasso in that journal of his." Offenbach published a weekly gossip sheet in German. "But he'll help you for a price. He cares only about money."

"In that case he's useless to me. I'm broke."

"Alice, my wallet, please."

Toklas stood slowly, as if she hoped that before she completed the action Stein would change her mind.

"Hurry, Alice—Hemingway's a busy man."

Toklas eased out of the room.

"I really can't take any money—"

"You're not taking. You're borrowing. I expect to be paid back in full."

"I don't know when—"

"When you're rich and famous. Isn't that what you want?"

"Isn't that what we all want?"

"Some more than others. You most of all. You have too much talent not to be successful."

Ernest was flattered. Stein's opinion was important to him. She was not generous with praise. He was about to get modest when Toklas reappeared, wallet in hand. Stein snapped it open, lifted out some bills and thrust them into Ernest's hands. He pocketed the money without counting it.

"Thank you. Thank you both."

Stein stood up, raising the hem of her tentlike kimono as she walked toward Ernest.

"Don't start gushing, Hemingway." She pecked him on the cheek. "Let us know what happens."

"I will."

"And give our love to Hadley."

Ernest aboutfaced. Toklas walked him to the door.

"That was a thousand francs we gave you."

Ernest looked down at the tiny woman, sick of her sarcasm, sick of her needling, sick of her jealousy. Tell her to mind her own business, tell her to go to hell, tell her to bug off. He wanted very much to tell her these things. But she was Miss Stein's best friend and he needed Miss Stein.

"I'll repay it. Thank you both for your generosity." Turning up his jacket collar, he left 27, rue de Fleurus.

CHAPTER 14

HARRY'S
SANK ROO DOE NOO

Ernest passed the sign in the front window of Harry's New York Bar and parted the saloon's swinging doors. Harry McElhone, the Scottish bartender who'd recently taken over the place, shook Ernest's hand and slapped him on the back. "Where you been hiding, Hem?"

"Switzerland." Ernest cocked a thumb towards the sign in the window. "What's with the phonetics?"

"I get tired of hearing everyone mispronouncing the address. That's what happens when you open a gin mill in Paris and everyone but the French patronize the place. Nobody can pronounce cinq rue Daunou."

"Business seems to be booming even without the French," said Ernest, surveying the three-deep bar through a thick haze of cigarette smoke.

"No complaints. What are you drinking?"

"Anything but a Bloody Mary."

Harry laughed heartily. One of the bar's claims to fame was having invented the tomato juice-vodka concoction dubbed the Bloody Mary. "I'll get you a beer."

"Thanks." Ernest threaded his way through the crowd. Three drunken college boys were standing on a table in a corner, trying to pin their alma mater's pennant to the wall. There were already too many damn pennants tacked up as far as Ernest was concerned. He had a good laugh when one of the college boys accidently thumbtacked his finger, lost his balance, and tumbled off the table, taking his friends with him.

At the next table sat Battling Siki, the Sengalese light heavyweight who had beaten Georges Carpentier, the French champ. Ernest admired Siki's style. Siki preferred training in saloons to gymnasiums. He also liked to march through Paris with his pet lion. Siki didn't have the lion in Harry's, but he did have a monkey on his shoulder. Two young women flanked him as he drank absinthe and fed peanuts to his pet.

A tired-looking blonde fell off her stool at the end of the bar. Ernest picked her up off the floor and plunked her back down. "Thansh, honey," she slurred, her breath aged in cheap whiskey.

"A noble gesture," said Owen O'Reilly, a friend of Ernest's who worked for the *Brooklyn Eagle*.

"I'm a regular knight-errant."

"Don't you know who that dame is?"

Ernest got only a quick second look before the blonde buried her head in her arms atop the bar. "Afraid not."

"Does the name Pearl White mean anything to you?"

"The actress from the *Perils of Pauline*?"

"One and the same. Her career in America fizzled out and she came here to get a fresh start." O'Reilly downed a shot of whiskey, then drenched his throat with a gulp of beer.

"I'd say it hasn't quite worked out for her."

"Yeah—she spends more time now hanging off bars than cliffs."

"Too bad."

"A bona fide American tragedy," said O'Reilly. "Can I get you a drink?"

"I have one coming. You haven't seen Louis Offenbach by any chance?"

"As a matter of fact, he followed me into the crapper a while ago. I told him if he wanted to yank a chain he'd have to go over to a fairy joint. He assured me that he was only interested in taking a shit. He's probably still there."

"Thanks."

"What do you want him for?"

"Some information."

O'Reilly was probably on his tenth boilermaker but his inherent reportorial instincts shone through his ossified state. "On a story, Ernie?"

"Come on, Owen. Offenbach only knows from Germans and your readers in Brooklyn never heard of Germany."

"You're a jaded bastard but I like you anyway." O'Reilly peered over Ernest's shoulder. "There's your man."

Ernest watched Offenbach come up the stairs. He was a short, curly-haired man whose ferretlike face was lined with deep middle-age wrinkles. He wore threadbare suits but smoked expensive Italian cigars. He kept a pen wedged atop his ear, ever ready to jot down the latest bit of Teutonic scandal. He wore white gloves which he removed only when writing notes on his hands.

"Hello, Louis."

Offenbach stepped back, afraid that Ernest might hit him again. "I've written nothing about you, Hemingway. Go away and let me do my job."

"All I want to do is buy you a drink."

Offenbach eyed him suspiciously. "Did someone put you up to this?"

Offenbach flinched as Ernest put his arm around him. "Louis, Louis, Louis. I'm deeply hurt. What happened between us was all a misunderstanding. Let's forget it, okay?" Ernest hoped that a little sweet talk might cut down Offenbach's price.

"We can sit at my table."

"Sure, Louis." Throwing a wink at O'Reilly, Ernest followed Offenbach to a small, round table in the back.

A waiter served Ernest's beer.

"What'll you have, Louis?"

"Champagne cocktail."

Ernest knew then that the Kraut bastard wasn't going to let him off cheap. "The gentleman will have a champagne cocktail," Ernest told the waiter.

"So, Louis, how's business?"

"*Comme ci, comme ça*. The economy is terrible in Germany so a lot of Germans are coming to Paris to look for work. But they've got no money and that's no good."

"Still you manage to survive."

Offenbach opened both hands, "I make ends meet."

I bet you do, you slimy bastard, thought Ernest. There was a rumor that Offenbach moonlighted as a blackmailer. "These are tough times for everyone," Ernest said.

The champagne cocktail arrived. It looked to Ernest like sparkling piss. "*À votre santé*," said Offenbach, raising his drink.

"Bottoms up." Ernest finished half his beer, smacking his lips just a little too loudly—he didn't want to overdo the conviviality routine.

"I was wondering, Louis, if you ever heard of a guy named Nicholas Burchardt."

Offenbach peeled off his gloves. His left hand was tattooed with notes. His right hand was spotless.

"What happens when there's no space left on your left hand?"

Offenbach snatched the pen from his ear. "I'm what you Americans call a switch-batter—"

"Switch-hitter."

"Whatever. I can write with either hand." He cribbed a message on the palm of his right hand.

"What's wrong with paper?"

"I'd lose it. This is better."

"Nicholas Burchardt," reminded Ernest.

"The name rings a bell but nothing more. Burchardt is not an uncommon name."

"What about a Russian named Beria?"

"Russians are pigs. They don't interest me."

"Then we have a problem, Louis. Both Burchardt and Beria interest me."

"Why?"

"Asked like a true reporter," said Ernest, cringing inwardly at playing up to Offenbach. "But I'd just as soon keep that particular intelligence to myself."

"Suit yourself." Offenbach wrote the names on his right hand. "Anything else?"

Ernest almost mentioned the Romanov papers and the German in the flier's coat. But he held back instinctively. He'd wait and see what Offenbach came up with on Beria and Burchardt.

"It will cost more than the price of a champagne cocktail," said Offenbach. Ernest left some francs on the table. "How much more?"

"That's hard to say. Gathering information like this is a delicate business. It takes finesse. And I don't know how long it will take."

"I'll give you a fair payment."

"Of course. But I could use a deposit."

"How much?"

Offenbach pulled on his gloves. "Let's say six hundred francs."

"Let's say forget it. That's fifty dollars." Ernest stood up angrily.

"Don't get so intemperate. I'll settle for five hundred francs."

Ernest dropped several bills on the table. "You'll settle for three hundred."

Offenbach whisked away the money with the speed and dexterity of a magician. "Where can I get in touch with you?"

"Sylvia Beach's bookstore."

"I'll do my best to help you."

"For that kind of money you better do better than best."

The bar had gotten more populated. Many of the new arrivals were English and American reporters Ernest knew. He had no time for fraternizing and rudely ignored a string of hellos as he walked out.

The twilight sky cast a pinkish hue over the city. A chill shot through him. He'd left his coat in the apartment. Walking up the rue Daunou, he debated whether to go back to his place, weighing the odds that his German pals would be waiting.

A sharp wind slicing down the street decided for him. He'd indulge himself and take a cab to the rue du Cardinal Lemoine, get out a few blocks away and scout the area. If it looked safe, he'd chance it and go in and get his coat.

The alternative was pneumonia and pneumonia was not a good way to die. Not at all his style.

Alone now at his table, Offenbach ordered another drink. What luck, he thought, that Hemingway should somehow be involved with Nicholas Burchardt—the late Nicholas Burchardt—and the Russian pig named Beria.

Offenbach had already been paid handsomely by the couple at the George V for information about Burchardt and Beria. He wouldn't have to lift a finger to answer Hemingway's questions—he could have told him right then. But why should he? Let the bastard wait, let him cool his toes, as the Americans would say.

In the meantime, Offenbach would see what more he could

find out about Burchardt, Beria, and the Grand Duchess Anastasia.

There was money to be made. And maybe even a chance at revenge—revenge against Hemingway.

Strinsky's good ear was achingly cold. "Damn," he said. "I knew they were after Hemingway."

"Stop complaining," said Proskumov, his mouth filled with half a chocolate *éclair*. "Would you rather be in Moscow? It's a hell of a lot colder there."

"At least no one stands outside for eight hours in winter."

Proskumov swallowed the *éclair*. After several years of working with the high-strung Strinsky, Proskumov had concluded that his partner was happy only when he had something to complain about and someone to listen. Proskumov was always willing to lend an ear, so to speak, as long as his enormous appetite was satiated.

Throughout the day, Proskumov had left Strinsky in the narrow alley diagonally across from Hemingway's apartment while he went on raids of the bakeries and cafes in the area. The food was cheap and good, at least compared with Russian food, which he detested. So he had no complaints. He sympathized with Strinsky, who had left only once to take a piss. Eight hours was a long time to stand in the cold and wait, especially if you didn't care whether you ate borscht or vichyssoise.

"We never should have lost Hemingway," said Strinsky.

"Our orders were to follow Hemingway. He got off the train and so did we. He went to his apartment. We stayed outside. How were we to know there were others after him?"

"We should have followed them up when they went up there."

"Stop with the 'we-should-haves.' We didn't. And we lost him."

"Beria will be mad as hell."

"What Beria doesn't know won't hurt him."

"So we wait for hours in the cold and we don't even know if he's coming back here."

Proskumov suddenly grabbed Strinsky and jerked him back, deeper into the alley. "Are you crazy?" Strinsky asked.

"Shut up! Someone's coming up the street."
"I don't see anyone."
"S-h-h . . . . Over there. Near the dance hall."
"Is it Hemingway?"

Blue and red light spilled into the street from the neon sign above the dance hall door. A man moved out of the shadows and darted into number 74.

"That was Hemingway," said Proskumov.
"Let's get him."
"For Christ's sake—our orders haven't changed. We wait."

A car idled past and parked at the corner. Strinsky and Proskumov backed into the alley.

"It's the Mercedes again," said Strinsky.
"I know. I can see that."

No one got out of the car.

"Can you make out how many are in there?"
"It's too dark."
"Goddamn it!" said Strinsky. "Those bastards are complicating things."
"*C'est la vie.*"
"What does that mean?"
"Don't you know anything?" asked Proskumov.
"I'd like to know what we're going to do."
"I told you—wait."
"Shit!"

Proskumov shrugged and devoured another *éclair*.

CHAPTER 15

Anastasia curled up on the bed like a child and covered her face in her hands.

She was frightened, confused, and tired. But she would not let herself cry. She had done too much of that in the past. Crying only made you weak. She couldn't afford the luxury of tears or self-pity.

Her diary rested on the pillow next to her. It had been months since she'd read it; years since she'd written in it. So much time had passed that she associated the diary with another person.

She had tried to read the diary earlier, but the entries had made her queasy, as if she were invading another's privacy. She had put the book down.

Now she wanted to read it. Her conviction, her belief in herself, was failing. She was filled with self-doubt. She needed to read the book—or at least a part of it—and remember again exactly what she had been through, exactly who she was. Reading the diary would be painful, but very necessary. It would keep away the tears.

Propping herself up on a pillow, she opened the diary to the middle and began to read:

July 26, 1918: I am alive, though I know very little as to how I survived the massacre. I do know that a soldier named Sergei saved me and brought me here—to the house of a doctor named Milchenkavitch in the town of Glda.

Glda is just forty miles from Ekaterinburg. Forty miles is too close to that horrible place.

July 27: Sergei and Dr. M. (I must save ink by using only the initial!) spent the last hour with me. I learned that Sergei's last name is Pargonsky and he is eighteen, only a year older than I. His hair is the color of wheat and he admitted that only recently did he start to shave. He is very shy.

The room I am in belonged to the doctor's late sister. The room is full of icons, which remind me of my mother.

The doctor told me that my injuries are serious but I will recover. He didn't know if there would be any scars. He said that I was unconscious for several days.

I asked Sergei how he saved me but Dr. M. said that I must rest. Reluctantly, I agreed. Before they left, they bowed. For the first time in my life, it seemed strange.

July 28: I had the nightmare again last night and screamed in my sleep. Dr. M. came. He didn't ask what my dream was about. I'm sure he knew. It is only natural that I dream a nightmare. After all, I lived one.

I have thought all morning of writing about the incident. I hate even to think about it, but at times I can think of little else. Perhaps I can exorcise the demons by putting everything on paper. Perhaps then the nightmares will go away. I must do something or I will go mad. I have no choice but to write. . . .

It began twelve days ago—July 16. Just past midnight. My sisters—Marie, Olga, and Tatiana—and I were asleep in our room on the second floor of the dreadful house in Ekaterinburg, the house which had been our prison for the last three months.

Yorovsky opened the door and turned on the light. "The White Army is getting close to the town," he said. "We will have to move you somewhere else."

Tatiana made a joke. "We'd be happy to stay here and wait for them."

Yorovsky was not amused. "Get dressed right away!" I hated Yorovsky. Of all the men in charge of guarding us since the revolution, he was the coldest, the cruelest.

I dressed slowly, so by the time I was ready, everyone else was waiting near the front door. My father was holding my little brother in his arms.

Yorovsky led us to the cellar and told us to wait. "The cars should be here in a few minutes." My father asked for some chairs and a soldier quickly brought three in and left.

My mother sat on one, my father on another. Holding Alexis, my father gently placed my brother's legs across the seat of the third chair.

No one spoke. After months of imprisonment, there was little to say. The maid, Demidova, was holding tightly to a small pillow, inside of which was sewn a box filled to the brim with jewels, the pitiful remains of the Romanov treasure.

The cellar was lit by two oil lamps, but even such dim illumination could not hide the effect of the revolution on my family. My father and mother looked years older; my sisters had lost their girlishness, their flirty charm. Even Alexis seemed to be maturing too quickly under the curse of hemophilia and the strain of seemingly endless imprisonment.

Five or ten minutes went by. I remember taking out a small crucifix and kissing the agonized figure of Christ. I prayed.

At that very moment, Yorovsky burst into the room, followed by a dozen soldiers carrying rifles.

"Your relatives tried to save you," Yorovsky said to my father. "They have failed. Now we must shoot you."

My father started out of his chair. Yorovsky raised his revolver and fired. Something warm—blood—sprayed against my face. My father collapsed.

The soldiers started to fire. I saw my sister Marie make the sign of the cross just as one of the soldiers shot her in the face.

I moved into the corner. Everyone was screaming. A bayonet split the pillow and impaled Demidova. Jewels spilled obscenely from the pillow.

Someone—I don't know who—fell against me and I fell to the floor. A bullet tore into my shoulder. A bayonet pierced my side.

The screaming stopped. I heard Alexis cry out my father's name. Two more shots were fired. Alexis was silent.

I was sure I was dying. My pain was excruciating. I prayed for death.

July 29: Sergei was here most of the afternoon. He told me that when the revolution broke out, his regiment mutinied and joined the Bolsheviks. His sympathies were always with the Whites, but he had no choice but to go along with the Bolsheviks.

He refused when I asked him to tell me how he had saved my life. "Dr. M. wants you to recover and not think of such things."

I begged him to tell me. He again refused. Finally, I ordered him to tell me. He had no choice.

He moved a chair closer to my bed. "My regiment was transferred to Ekaterinburg a month ago. We were told something important was going to happen, but nobody said what. We thought we might have to escort the royal family to another town. The night of the . . . murders, we were ordered to the Czar's house. I was frightened, because by that time there were rumors that the Romanovs had been executed. We came in two trucks. We were taken to the cellar and . . . and . . . God . . ." He stopped, overwhelmed by the memory of what he had seen. "I'm sorry. We were told to take the bodies upstairs. Another soldier and I carried you into one of the trucks. Then they told us to go back into the house and get the suitcases and boxes. I found a small case and opened it. There were papers in it, papers with your name on them. I wanted to bring the case to you. I don't know why. I thought you were dead, but I wanted you to have it. So I went back to the truck and put the case next to you. That's when you moved, just a bit. First I thought I was seeing things but your fingers moved and I felt your heart beating. I covered you with a blanket so that no one would see that you were still alive."

I had forgotten about the suitcase, forgotten about the documents, forgotten about the photographs of my family, the letters from my father, the date book, the Bible with the sealed entries of my baptism and first communion. For no good reason I had assumed that only this diary had survived. "Where is the suitcase?"

"In the doctor's office. Do you want it?"

"Not now. I want to know how you got me away from the Bolsheviks."

"I was ordered to ride in the back of the truck, the second truck, so there was no one following. I ripped some shirts I found in one of the suitcases and made bandages. About ten miles from Ekaterinburg, the trucks stopped, there was something blocking the road. I took a chance and carried you out of the truck and left you in the woods. Then I got back in the truck and we went down the road some more until we reached a clearing that had been picked for the burial."

"Didn't anyone notice that my body was missing? Weren't there any officers?"

"There were officers, but they were all drunk. So were most of the soldiers. I helped carry the bodies from the trucks. I had stuffed a coat with clothing and rags and anything else I could find and I carried the coat out. In the dark, everyone assumed it was just another body. There was too much confusion, they were too busy doing other things." Sergei looked away from me and said nothing more.

"What things?"

"It's done—there's no reason to tell you."

"I have a right to know."

"Please—"

"They were my family. I want to know what was done to them."

"Their bodies were burned." I sensed that he was not telling everything but I did not press the point. He took a glass of water and continued: "There isn't much else to tell. There was too much confusion and too many drunks to notice what had happened to you. One of the officers tried to make a check and he asked me who had burned your body. I said I had. He told me that I was now a part of Russian history. I wanted to kill him—I wanted to kill them all. Finally, I just ran away. I went first into Koptyaki, the nearest town, and made arrangements for a carriage. Then I went back to get you."

"Do you think the Bolsheviks know?"

"They shouldn't. The man who came with the carriage is an old friend. He swore not to talk of what he had seen. And the doctor is quite famous in these parts for his loyalty to the Czar. He'll say nothing."

"Does that mean we're safe?"

Sergei absently picked up an icon from the table and studied it. "You'll never be safe in Russia. We'll never make it to the White Army lines—it's too dangerous. And the Cheka is everywhere. Sooner or later, they'll catch us. We can't stay in Russia."

"When must we leave?"

"As soon as you can travel. The doctor doesn't want you

moved for three weeks. I don't think we can wait more than one."

I doubted that I would feel much better by then, but I didn't want Sergei to know. "I'm sure I'll be able to travel."

Sergei bowed. "I am Russian," he said. "And you are Russia."

I began to cry. Sergei reached over, hesitated, then tentatively, gently, stroked my hair.

August 14: We have stopped at a village near the Rumanian border. It is raining and a farmer and his wife have taken us in for the night and fed us. They have little, but what they have they share.

We left Dr. M.'s a week ago. We have been traveling southwest toward Rumania. Sergei has relatives in Bucharest and he thinks they will help us get to Berlin, where many Whites are said to be living.

We have been telling people that we are brother and sister, leaving Russia to start a new life. The last part, at least, is not a lie. These people do not ask questions—in fact, they have not yet heard of the revolution and they still speak of the Czar as their leader. It is terribly sad.

It is getting late now. Sergei is sleeping in the barn. I miss him most at night, when we are apart. I know it is wrong, but I want him to touch me, to make love to me.

God has allowed me to live. I pray he will forgive me these thoughts.

September 19: Today we reached Bucharest. Outside the city, we sold the horse and carriage. We are rich! No, not really rich, but at least able to afford an inexpensive hotel while Sergei gets in touch with his uncle and aunt.

After so many months' imprisonment, the sight of a city is overwhelming. Bucharest is nothing like St. Petersburg (what is?) but there are restaurants and shops and theatres, none of which we can afford but all of which fill me with joy. It is wonderful to watch Sergei, who has never been to a place larger than Ekaterinburg. He is so boyish, I want to hug him and love him. But still, he has not come to me.

September 20: A bad day and a beautiful one. Sergei went to his uncle's home and discovered that both his uncle and aunt had died. There is no one else. When he came back to the hotel, he was so dejected! I put my arms around him and told him I loved him. He said he loved me but hadn't dared confess his feelings since he was a lowly soldier and I the grand duchess.

I kissed him and we went to bed. We were awkward—it was the first time for us both.

Sergei says he wants to marry me. I tell him I want to wait and get to know him better and we both laugh. I know we did nothing wrong, but still I pray—asking forgiveness and thanking God for bringing Sergei to me.

September 26: Sergei is again worried that the Bolsheviks are looking for us. He says someone followed him yesterday. I doubt that anything is amiss but he insists that we leave Rumania. To make him happy, I agree.

October 4: We arrived three days ago in Belgrade with just enough money to rent a squalid little flat. Sergei is looking for work but so far has had no success. Each day he grows more despondent. Our only comfort is our love.

October 7: A wonderful day—Sergei found a job working in the kitchen of a restaurant. We will not become wealthy but we will be able to save enough to eventually get to Berlin.

January 3, 1919: I've begun to feel like a prisoner in this flat. Sergei does not want me to go out for fear that I might be recognized—he worries that Bolsheviks are everywhere. Sometimes, when he is at work, I walk to the pleasant little park nearby and watch the children play. But usually I honor his wishes and stay home, reading the German and Russian books he occasionally finds in a secondhand bookstore.

The time passes slowly. We are hoping to leave for Berlin next month. I wish I could go to sleep tonight and wake up and it would be February.

February 12: Next week, Berlin! We have saved practically all of Sergei's salary and we are almost ready.

March 3: We arrived in Berlin yesterday. We have little money left after our journey and we have had to take a terrible room on the Rudenstrasse, in the worst part of the city. Sergei must find work. Tomorrow I will visit the White Russian community.

March 7: No one will see me. I have been to the homes of the Russian elite in Berlin and everywhere I was rebuffed. Servants refuse to let me enter, none will tell their master or mistress who I am. They all call me mad. Tomorrow I visit the home of Count Vladimir Koblinski, one of my father's closest friends. Surely he will see me. Surely he will know who I am.

March 8: My visit with the count was a failure. I never thought he would deny me. Yet he did, calling me "insane" and a "lunatic." I begged him to tell the others who I am. He refused. "The Romanovs are dead—you are an impostor," he said. He dismissed the photographs, the letters, the Bible as "meaningless, forgeries, or stolen from the grave." He ordered me to leave. I am ashamed to say that I cried and asked him to reconsider. "A true grand duchess would never act in such a manner," he said, and closed the door on me.

What will Sergei and I do?

March 10: We left our hotel in the middle of the night, unable to pay our bill. There is no work for Sergei, perhaps no future at all for us. We slept last night in a church. This morning, the sacristan found us and ordered us away, threatening to call the police if we ever returned.

Where will we go?

March 12: A miracle in the unlikeliest place (at least for a Christian like me)—a synagogue.

The night before last was especially cold and windy. Sergei and I walked the streets for hours until I could go on no more. We found ourselves in front of a grand synagogue on . . . I forget the street. The building was locked. Sergei picked up a large rock and broke open a side door. We went inside and quickly fell asleep.

Hours later, a rough hand against my shoulder awakened me. It was a rabbi, and he said he was going to call the police. I told him in German that we had no place to go. He wasn't interested. I could sense that Sergei—who speaks only

Russian—was on the verge of silencing the rabbi, perhaps forever.

I didn't know what to do.

Then the miracle happened.

A man, a well-dressed, middle-aged man, appeared and interceded. He listened to my tale of destitution, then told me in perfect Russian that he would pay for the damages and assuage the rabbi's anger. He did exactly that and then invited us to the cafe across the street. He bought us breakfast—our first meal in three days.

Over coffee, he told us that although he was Russian-born he had come to Germany years ago to seek his fortune. This he had found and he was now a successful manufacturer.

What, he asked, was our story?

I hesitated, unsure that he would believe me, unsure that I could trust him. But something about him told me that he was a good man. I decided I could trust him.

For the next thirty minutes, I told him who I was and how I had come to Berlin. At first, he did not believe me. I was not surprised. I produced the documents. He was obviously impressed, but he repeated Count Koblinski's suspicion that the documents were either forged or stolen.

I told him about my family, about the Romanovs. I spoke in French and English. Embarrassed, he admitted that he could speak neither language.

He was intrigued. He said he didn't really believe my story but admitted that he was . . . interested. He invited us to his home. We gladly accepted.

His name is Nicholas Burchardt.

He lives outside Berlin in a fine house with his family and several servants (two of his maids are Russian!). His children—a son and daughter—are the same age as Sergei and I. Like their father, they are kind and generous. Frau Burchardt is a quiet woman but also very nice.

Burchardt is beginning to believe my story. The possibility that he is sheltering the Czar's daughter amuses him, and, I think, makes him proud.

Tonight he asked me what I plan to do in the future.

"Nothing," I said.

"But why? If you are who you say you are, don't you want to rally your people?" He was testing me.

"I want nothing to do with them after what they did for me. Not after their rejection. I need time to heal."

He smiled. "You're welcome to stay here as long as you like," he said, kissing my hand. "We are honored."

Anastasia threw the diary across the room, fighting the tears. She knew that without Nicholas Burchardt she would not have survived. He had saved her life, and Sergei's. He had made them live again.

He had done everything for her, including die.

She thought about him, his wife, his children. No one had ever been kinder. Only her own parents had loved her more. And they were dead.

Just like Burchardt.

And it was her fault.

She wanted to cry but did not. Reading the diary had at least accomplished something. She would shed no more tears.

CHAPTER 16

Statues of two squat Chinese dignitaries lorded over the brightly lit Café des Deux Magots, their faces peering down as some two dozen customers sipped *café au lait* or nursed harder—and more expensive—refreshments.

Ernest pushed through the café's revolving door at precisely 7:45 P.M.—fifteen minutes before his date with Renata Lande. He hadn't had much chance to think about her during the day, but as he had walked to the Deux Magots from his apartment he had questioned her seemingly innocent and charming appearance the night before on the *Orient Express*.

After all, she was German, and so were the men who had kidnapped him. She just might be caught up in the whole mess, just might be able to help him. He wanted her to keep the date with him; even if she had nothing to do with the missing manuscripts, he wanted to see her again. She was so damn attractive.

Ernest got a beer at the bar and took a look around to see if he knew anyone. He drew a blank except for a middle-aged man who sat alone at a table in the far corner. Grabbing his beer, Ernest sidled through the closely set tables and approached James Joyce.

"I was taught that when an Irishman drinks by himself he's either getting ready to beat someone up or kill himself." Ernest stood on the other side of the tiny table, just three feet from Joyce.

"Is that you, Hemingway?" Joyce's eyes squinted up at Ernest through lenses thick as magnifying glasses.

"It is. Would you like company for a few minutes?"

"The honor is mine entirely." Joyce snatched away his cane from the opposite chair so Ernest could sit.

Joyce's face was gentle, yet cunning; his frame thin and wiry. He reminded Ernest of the Jack of Spades—dark, moustached, brooding. A Jack of Spades going blind, thought Ernest.

"How have you been?" asked Ernest.

"Bad, very bad—or so say the medicine men who claim to be my physicians."

Health—specifically his own poor health—was a popular subject with Joyce. Ernest often wondered how Joyce had found time between complaints to write *Ulysses*.

"I need another operation on my eyes—"

Ernest started to sympathize but Joyce had more to say. "And they want to yank my teeth out as well." Joyce's smile justified his dentist's diagnosis. "An 'eye for an eye, a tooth for a tooth.' I may not be able to see without my eyes but I sure as hell can drink without my teeth." He finished his dry sherry and raised a hand for another.

"When are you having the operation?"

"I leave tomorrow evening for Berlin."

"Why Berlin?"

Joyce laughed as if he were trying to clear his nose. "There's yet another so-called miracle surgeon who's perfected a new technique. I'm afraid I've met too many of these chaps already. But you always hope. . . ."

A gust of cold air blew into the café as two men, one considerably taller than the other, came through the door and sat down at a nearby table. Ernest recognized them immediately. They were the men from the Lausanne train station last night. What were they doing in the Deux Magots? Coincidence? Possible but unlikely. Ernest shifted in his seat so he could keep an eye on them.

"Have you been to the Comédie-Française lately?" asked Joyce.

"Afraid not."

"I went the other day. Couldn't see it of course but it was marvelous just to listen to the actors."

The mention of actors reminded Ernest of seeing Pearl White in Harry's. He told Joyce the story.

"Pearl White? Is she the poor girl who's always jumping around in those films they call cliff-hangers?"

"The one and the same."

"What's she doing in Paris?"

"Trying to find work. She's all washed up back in the States."

"I thought Americans in Paris were interested only in writing."

"Maybe she should write. She's not getting much work here."

"Of course she should." Joyce encored his yellow smile. "She could write a *roman à clef-hanger*."

Ernest laughed politely, thinking he'd never been terribly fond of puns. He looked in the mirror behind Joyce. Someone was pushing through the revolving door. It was Renata.

She was wrapped in a tight blue coat and her dark hair swirled over a fur collar. She looked beautiful. Ernest waved and stood. "A friend of mine is joining us," he said.

"Male or female?"

"Female."

"Splendid," said Joyce.

Renata stopped in the middle of the cafe. Her eyes darted from Ernest to the two men from Lausanne. So she recognizes them, too, thought Ernest. He'd been right: their appearance was not a coincidence. Renata backed away, turned, and ran out of the Deux Magots.

"Is she here yet?" asked Joyce.

"She was."

"Was? She certainly didn't stay very long."

The two men hurriedly got up and started off.

"Wait a minute," Ernest said.

The shorter man ignored Ernest and walked away. The taller man followed. Ernest lunged at him, gripping his right sleeve. "Where are you going?" he asked. "What's the rush?" The man jerked Ernest's hand away.

"I want to talk to you," said Ernest.

The shorter man was already at the door. The other man started to run. "Hold it," said Ernest, blocking his way. The man hit Ernest in the stomach and knocked the wind out of him.

"Take care of him, Hemingway," coaxed Joyce, flailing his cane in the air. "Take care of him."

"He's not here anymore," groaned Ernest as he rushed outside. The tall man was racing down the rue Bonaparte toward the Seine. Ernest ran after him.

At the end of the narrow rue Bonaparte, Ernest skimmed

down a flight of stone steps to the Quai Voltaire. A young man and woman broke their embrace to watch Ernest as he sprinted after the tall man, who was at least fifty yards ahead. "*Mes apologies*," Ernest said to the couple.

The quai was dark, with only faint light coming from the street lamps on the street above. Trees lined the quai to Ernest's right. To his left was the Seine, and beyond the river the Louvre.

The taller man seemed to be slowing. Ernest could barely discern another figure farther along the quai. He couldn't tell if it was the tall man's companion or Renata.

Within seconds he knew where the shorter man was. The man suddenly leaped at Ernest from the shadows and tackled him to the ground. The man smelled terrible, like week-old *bouillabaisse*. He pummeled Ernest's face, reopening the split lip. Blood filled Ernest's mouth. Ernest slammed his fists against the man's head, then brought his knees up and kicked the man off. Ernest jumped to his feet, locked his hands together and swung them into the man's face. Blood spurted and the man fell back, one hand covering his nose, the other scraping against the cobblestones to break his fall. Ernest stood over him.

"Get up, you son of a bitch!"

The man seemed hurt but not frightened and he looked away from Ernest and peered down the quai. Ernest whirled around, figuring the tall man was on the attack. He was. Barreling into Ernest, the tall man hooked an arm across Ernest's neck and forced Ernest's right arm up behind his back, jamming it upward so the hand was touching the base of his shoulder blade.

The short man got up slowly. Blood rolled down his chin. The tall man tightened his grip around Ernest's neck, then handed his partner a knife. The short man pressed a button on the handle and a long, thin blade clicked open. The tall man lowered his arm a bit so his friend could touch the tip of the blade to Ernest's Adam's apple.

"You don't need that," said Ernest. "Your breath is foul enough to kill anyone."

The man moved the blade along Ernest's throat, stopping just below the jawbone. His hold tightened on the knife, readying to shove the blade into Ernest's throat.

Blood from the sliced lip filled Ernest's mouth. He remembered an old club fighter's trick, swallowed the blood halfway, then brought it back into his mouth and spit into the short man's eyes. Momentarily blinded, the man stumbled back a few feet, rubbing his coat sleeve against his eyes. Ernest shot his right leg up like a punter's, kicking the short man in the balls. The man dropped the knife and hunched over, his moans echoing along the quai.

The tall man started to break Ernest's arm, pulling it up, nearly snapping it at the elbow. Ernest bowed his head, as if he had passed out, then whipped his head back and butted the tall man in the face.

Stunned, the man released Ernest and backed away. Ernest stooped over to pick up the short man's knife. Before he got it, the tall man smashed into him, digging his hands around his neck. Ernest planted his own hands flat against the tall man's face and pushed. The tall man's stranglehold tightened. Suddenly, Ernest tore his hands from the man's face and quickly sent a series of sharp rabbit punches to the man's kidneys. The man grunted and loosened his hold. Ernest chopped the side of his right hand into the man's neck. Finally, the tall man let go of Ernest.

But the tall man wasn't through yet. He took several swings at Ernest, clipping him once painfully on the cheek. Ducking low to dodge the punches, Ernest hit the man twice in the gut, then brought his arm up and cracked him in the jaw. Bits of teeth flew from the man's mouth.

Still, he wouldn't go down. He stepped closer and went for Ernest's stomach. Ernest sank his left hand into the man's lapel and snapped six punches to the right side of the man's head. On the last shot, the man's ear fell off!

The tall man fell against Ernest and rolled to the ground.

Exhausted, Ernest leaned against a tree. "Want some more, you son of a bitch? Get up!" The man didn't budge.

Ernest reached down and picked up the mangled ear. It was wax. Ernest pitched it into the Seine.

At some point, the short man had disappeared. Ernest looked up and down the quai, saw nothing, then bent over the tall man and started going through his pockets. He heard a noise from behind. He turned. The short man had sneaked back, a sap raised in his hand.

Ernest started up, but the blackjack caught him across the

back of the head. Ernest fell to his knees, wavered. His vision blurred. The sap came down again. Ernest hit the ground and passed out.

A dog's tongue lapped at Ernest's face. Ernest groggily shoved the dog away, opened one eye a crack. His first thought was that he was blind, but a light twinkled from across the river and he realized that it was still night and that probably very few minutes had passed since he'd been knocked out. The dog—a scraggly mutt with a drooling mouth—renewed his licking.

"Beat it, you dirty bastard." Ernest slowly brought himself into a sitting position. The dog backed off a few steps. "Go away—*Fous-moi!*" The dog barked once and trotted off.

Ernest's head—or what was left of it—throbbed with a pain worse than a hundred hangovers. Several bumps caked with blood had sprouted on his scalp. He crawled five feet to the edge of the quai and vomited. That at least made him feel that he was not going to die within the next few minutes.

He struggled to his feet. There was no sign of the two men. His guess was that they had figured he was dead and so had taken off. But they hadn't bargained on the Hemingway skull, one of the thickest specimens in the world, or so he liked to think. At the moment, it was certainly one of the most painful.

He walked slowly along the quai, trying to make some sense of a situation that was becoming more senseless every minute. Who the hell were the two men? What was their connection to Renata Lande? And who really cares? thought Ernest, especially when my head feels like a son of a bitch.

He went up the ramp to the Boulevard St.-Michel, weaving as if he were drunk. Several passersby snickered as he reached out for a street lamp, breathing hard and trying his damndest not to puke.

Two green lights came and went before he felt confident enough to cross the boulevard and walk the four blocks to the police station on the rue Parcheminerie.

On the way, he thought about Renata and the two men in the Deux Magots. Why had she run? Did she know them? Or did she simply recognize them from the train station? Who were they following?

While his aching head rebelled against such musing, he concluded that Renata was afraid of something and had run from those two men because she recognized them. While the evidence might be skimpy, he decided that she had to be involved in the theft of his manuscripts.

He stopped outside the red brick building, brushing dirt from his coat and pants, making himself look as presentable as possible; he didn't want the Paris police thinking he was some crazy whose tale of attempted murder was inspired by the full moon.

The scene inside the police station reminded him of similar scenes he'd witnessed as a reporter in Kansas City. Three drunks slept on the floor, a tourist frantically told a flic about the theft of his wallet, and an old woman cried about her son's accidental death. Ernest approached a cop who seemed to be the least harried.

"I want to report an attempted murder."

"Murders, successful or not, are Inspector Dupré's affair."

"Where is Dupré?"

The cop pointed to a door behind Ernest. "In his office."

Ernest knocked twice. No reply.

"He hates to be disturbed," said the cop. "He's a busy man."

"Oh yeah? What's he busy with?"

"His dinner. He's so busy that he eats at his desk."

"I hope he likes to work there, too," said Ernest, pushing open the door. A man was bent over, rummaging through a wicker basket on the floor. His backside was wide and mountainous, the ass of a man who spent most of his life behind a desk, concerned more with his piles than crime in Paris.

"Is that you, Pesce? I told you I wanted no disturbances." Dupré did not turn around.

"My name is Hemingway. I'm an American. And I don't like talking to asses."

Inspector Dupré straightened up and turned. He was an ordinary-looking, middle-aged man whose most distinctive feature was a prominent mole on the tip of his nose. Several hairs blossomed from the mark. "Who are you?"

"I just told you. Ernest Hemingway. I work for the International News Service. I want to report an attempted murder."

"Whose?"

"Mine."

Dupré rubbed his hirsute mole. "I see." He picked up the wicker basket, walked around his desk and sat down.

"I'm damn happy that you see, Inspector. Maybe you'll see even better when I give you a few facts."

Dupré opened the basket and took out a bottle of wine, a glass, a loaf of bread, and a square of *pâté*. With a letter opener he cut several slices of bread, which he smeared with *pâté*. Then he uncorked the wine and filled his glass. He ate a piece of bread and washed it down with a sip of wine. "What facts would you be speaking of?"

Ernest controlled his rising anger and told the story he'd told to Gertrude Stein, updating it to include the attack along the quai. Through it all, Dupré ate his dinner of cold chicken, green salad, and cheese. He finished his meal just as Ernest finished the story. "Are those all the facts?" asked Dupré, wiping his chin with a napkin.

"Isn't that enough?"

"*Absolument*—more than enough."

"So what are you going to do?"

"Hopefully, relax for a moment and put an end to this rather common wine my wife maliciously packed for me."

"What about what you just heard?"

"Monsieur . . ."

"Hemingway."

"Monsieur Hemingway. I work long and tiring hours. My wife has, for reasons unknown to me, become a religious fanatic who actually prays for my death so she will be free to enter the convent. My one joy in life is my dinner and you have just ruined it with this ridiculous story."

Ernest angrily slammed his fist down on Dupré's desk. A chicken bone bounced out of the basket and dropped on the floor. "What I told you was true."

"Please, monsieur, the desk is older than I and in even worse condition," Dupré said. "Your valise may very well be gone. Stolen. Lost. Whatever. These things happen. And apartments—especially in your quarter—are ripe for plucking, particularly when the tenants are away."

"What about the two men at the quai?"

"Criminals—Paris has its share. Perhaps you would feel safer back in America."

"You're not going to do anything, are you?"

"Monsieur, try to see it from my position. I am understaffed. One of my best men is out sick. And there has already been one murder tonight."

"When?"

"I don't know. A body was discovered in the Seine. I'm going there in a few minutes."

"You don't believe in rushing into things, do you, Inspector?"

"The dead stay dead. Now, if you'll excuse me." Dupré reached for a coat hanging from a nail in the wall.

"I'd like to go with you."

"Why?"

"I'm a reporter. Maybe there's a story." That was bullshit. Ernest wanted to tag alone to see if the corpse was someone he knew—someone like Renata Lande.

Dupré ushered Ernest out of his office. "Corpses in the Seine are as common as whores in Pigalle. Although . . ."

"Although what, Inspector?"

They exited the police station and turned toward the river. "Well," said Dupré, "corpses usually pop up in the spring. Warm weather apparently makes them float to the surface."

"This is December. Maybe this is special."

Dupré sighed, the world-weary European quickly losing patience with the pushy American. "If I let you come, will you promise not to harass me anymore with that absurd story of yours?"

"There's nothing absurd about it."

Dupré stopped abruptly. "Monsieur, do you want to come or not?"

"Lead on—I won't say another word."

They walked to the river in silence. The throbbing ache in Ernest's head was slowly diminishing, but he still had trouble keeping up with Dupré's pace. At the Quai St.-Bernard, Dupré cut across a barren knoll to the river. There was no seawall and water slopped over the low hedge of stones that had been constructed hundreds of years before.

Two gendarmes and a man Ernest took for a doctor stood over a body that was covered partially by a dark coat. Dupré nodded to the trio and knelt over the body, pulling away the coat.

The corpse was a man's. The face was bloodless, the eyes

closed, the mouth open in a silent scream of agony. The man had been cut open from his stomach to his chest.

"He smells worse than a hard-boiled egg," Dupré looked up at the doctor. "So?"

The doctor seemed confused. "So?"

"So why didn't he sink? It's freezing out and he should have sunk."

The doctor prodded the dead man's right shoulder. A six-inch gash in the man's coat ran from the shoulder to the top of the arm. "He was caught on one of the mooring hooks on the other side of the wall." The hooks were used by fishermen to tie up their boats.

Dupré quickly searched the dead man's pockets. He found nothing but a piece of black cloth emblazoned with a strange red symbol in the middle. Dupré unfurled the cloth. "He had terrible taste in handkerchiefs."

Ernest said nothing.

Dupré stood up and glanced across the river at a uninspired red brick building—the Paris morgue. "*Suivez la Seine jusqu'à la morgue*," he said, reciting the first line of an ancient children's song. "Follow the Seine to the morgue." The gendarmes and the doctor chuckled.

"I guess I'll be on my way," Ernest said.

"Our vivisected friend doesn't interest you?" asked Dupré.

"Just another dead man." Ernest pocketed the pad and pencil he had taken out for appearances' sake. His fingers brushed against something in his pocket. He took the object out. It was the second cigar Sara Morgan had given him the night he took on the mad Turk. "I'm sorry to have troubled you, Inspector. I'd be honored if you accepted this as a token of my appreciation."

Dupré beamed at the gendarmes. "A good policeman never accepts a bribe but he also never declines a good cigar. *Merci, monsieur.*"

Ernest wanted to stay and see the expression on Dupré's face when the cigar exploded, but he couldn't afford a night in jail. "Goodbye, Inspector," he said and quickly walked away. He felt pleased for the first time in days.

The reason for his good mood was not the exploding cigar— though that was a good enough trick—but the cloth that Dupré had discovered on the body. It wasn't a handkerchief.

It was a torn armband, black and decorated with a blood-red, twisted cross. A swastika.

The last time Ernest had seen it was during a political rally in Germany—a rally held by the National Socialist party. The dead man on the quai was a Nazi.

Things were beginning to fall into place. The Germans—Pilot, Nose, and the others who'd abducted him—were Nazis, just like the floater from the Seine. The Nazis were looking for the Romanov documents, whatever the hell they were.

For some reason, they thought he had them, or knew where they were.

Why?

Here it got murky. Someone had taken his manuscripts. Not the Germans, if The Pilot was to be believed. "We inherited them," he had said.

From whom?

Burchardt? Beria? Renata Lande?

Clearly, whoever it was had taken the manuscripts by mistake. Someone had killed the Nazi, perhaps because he had the Romanov documents. Had he been on his way to the Gare de Lyon to deliver the papers?

Ernest didn't have those answers, yet. But he'd get them.

CHAPTER 17

The Shakespeare and Company bookstore usually closed around seven but Sylvia Beach was still there when Ernest tapped on the front window at nine-thirty.

Sylvia poked her pretty face out the front door. Her vibrant brown eyes sized up Ernest severely. "If you didn't look so terrible I'd tell you that tonight's my inventory night and we're closed."

"But I look terrible."

"Worse than that." She threw open the door. "Come on in."

"Did I ever tell you that you've got great legs?"

"About forty times. But don't ever stop."

Ernest made himself comfortable in a padded chair next to the big, pot-bellied stove that sat in front of the fireplace. The bookstore, its walls decorated with photos of famous and obscure writers, was one of his favorite places, its proprietress one of his favorite people.

Sylvia had been kind and generous to him ever since he'd first met her. He borrowed heavily from her lending library and spent long hours in the store, browsing and discussing books with Sylvia.

"There's blood on your jacket."

"I cut my noggin. Nothing serious."

"You weren't the only one in the Red Cross." Sylvia had served with the RC in Belgrade during the war. "And your lip is bashed. Let me have a look."

As she examined his scalp, Ernest skimmed a three-week-old copy of the *The New York Times Book Review*. He stopped at an ad for a new novel by Edith Wharton called *A Son at the Front*. Ernest one day planned to write *the* war novel, but the ad didn't bother him. His novel would be the best war novel anyone ever wrote, with the possible exception of Mr. Tolstoi. "Are my brains showing?"

"No danger of that with such a hard head." Sylvia went into a rear stockroom. "I'll clean up your scrapes and you can tell me how you got them."

Ernest glanced at Joyce's photo above the mantle. Sylvia had recently published *Ulysses*. "I ran into Joyce. He was well on his way to an historic drunk."

Sylvia carried in a pan of steaming water, a rag, and a bottle of hydrogen peroxide. "He's terribly worried about his eyes. Who wouldn't be?" She doused the cuts with the peroxide and dabbed the rag against his scalp. "Now tell me how your head got in such a sorry state."

"It's a long story that gets longer with every telling."

"You need practice with longer narratives, no matter what Gertrude Stein thinks. Tell me all."

He told her about the stolen manuscripts, the ransacked apartment, the kidnapping and escape, the aborted rendezvous at the Deux Magots with Renata Lande, the fight with the two men along the quai, and the dead Nazi in the river.

"It sounds like something from a John Buchan novel," she said when he was through.

"Except *The 39 Steps* makes more sense."

"What do you think is going on?"

"Well, my manuscripts were stolen from the Gare de Lyon. The Nazis are looking for the Romanov documents. The dead Nazi could have been delivering the documents to someone at the station but was killed before he got there. Whoever was waiting for the documents could have snatched my manuscripts by mistake. Maybe the suitcases looked alike."

"So who has the Romanov documents?"

"The Nazis wanted to know about Burchardt and Beria, so those two are the likely candidates. So is Renata Lande. I don't think our meeting on the train was merely a pleasant accident. Maybe they're all involved in a struggle with the Nazis over these mysterious Romanov documents."

Sylvia splashed peroxide on Ernest's lip. "Of course, it could always be coincidence."

"I don't believe in that these days."

Sylvia completed her ministrations. "What are you going to do now?"

"Have a drink, if you've got anything in this joint worth drinking."

"You'll have to settle for tea."

Ernest rubbed his hands in front of the stove. "That sounds terrible but I'll take it."

Sylvia headed back into the stockroom to brew a pot.

Ernest cracked his knuckles and stretched his legs. *A Book of Burlesques* by H. L. Mencken sat on Sylvia's desk, reminding him of Sara Morgan and her tempting offer: a good salary and a sound newspaper job back in the States. Did he want it? No. But could he afford to refuse? He and Hadley wanted kids someday. And he didn't want Hadley to live in squalor the rest of her life. Hell, he was no fan of poverty. But there had to be a better way than a job with the Allied News Service. He had to write his way out of it, do it his way. And he had to have his stories back.

The phone on Sylvia's desk was ringing.

"Could you get that, Ernest? My hands are full."

"Sure." Ernest picked up the phone. "Shakespeare and Company. Contract killers."

A crackling noise like a thunderstorm came over the line.

"You'll have to speak up," said Ernest. "The connection is bad."

More static. Then: "Ernest, is that you?"

"Hadley? Christ!"

"When are you coming back?"

Rain dappled the window. Sylvia set a cup of tea on a box next to his chair. Someone knocked on the door.

"I should be back tomorrow. But I can't say for sure."

Sylvia was talking to someone. Ernest cupped a hand over his ear, straining to hear Hadley over the static and Sylvia's conversation.

"I couldn't sleep last night, Ernest. I kept thinking about what I'd done, how stupid I was."

"Forget it, kiddo. The stuff'll turn up."

Ernest heard the door close. Sylvia nudged him on the shoulder. He swiveled in his seat. Renata Lande stood in the middle of the bookstore. She tossed her head a bit, sprinkling raindrops on the floor.

"I love you, Ernest," Hadley said.

Staring at Renata while he spoke to Hadley made him feel

guilty. Very guilty. "We'll go bankrupt with this call," he said.

"Didn't I tell you? Mr. Steffens is paying for it. He's such a dear."

"He is, but let's not bankrupt him either."

"You're right. Promise me you'll try to come back tomorrow."

"I'll try."

"I love you."

"Me too," Ernest said and hung up.

Renata tried out a smile but quickly saw that Ernest was not receptive. "I'm sorry about the scene in the cafe."

The one thing Ernest didn't want to do was lose his temper. But he did. "You're sorry! Hey, that's terrific. No problem." His voice rose with each word. He stood up angrily. "Those two friends of yours were swell company. We ended up at the river and they almost killed me. One of them had a knife and the other had an ear that fell off. They were a real comedy team. You should have stayed around to enjoy the show."

Sylvia positioned herself between them like a referee at a prize fight. "There's no need to shout, Ernest."

"Sorry. It's just that I almost got killed tonight and I don't have one goddamn good reason why."

Sylvia turned to Renata. "Would you like some tea?"

"If it's no trouble."

"No trouble at all." Sylvia moved past Ernest and went into the back room.

"How did you find me here?" asked Ernest.

"You told me last night on the train that you often came here. I didn't expect you here. I was just going to leave a message."

"Was your message going to include an explanation?"

"I was hoping to explain in person."

"Well, my person is here—a little bruised but still functioning."

Renata took off her coat. Ernest tried thinking of Hadley.

"Do you remember in the train I told you about my friend in Lausanne?"

"The painter?"

"Yes. What I didn't tell you is that he's married. His wife is quite wealthy."

Ernest was sure he was being set up. "Don't tell me," he

said. "He promised he'd divorce his wife. Only you finally realized he never would and decided to leave him."

"Do you treat everyone like a character in one of your stories?"

"I just don't like being played for a sucker. That story is a little hackneyed. If you want sympathy, you'll have to do better than that. "

"That was your version—not mine. The truth is that Marcel—"

"Marcel?"

"The painter, the married man. Marcel told me he was going to get a divorce. I told him not to. I told him I didn't love him anymore. I was the one who ended it."

"That's an interesting twist. But it still doesn't explain why you ran out of the Deux Magots and why those two thugs damn near killed me."

"They were hired by Marcel. They were on the *Orient Express*."

That part, at least, was true. Those two characters had been in the waiting room in Lausanne. "Why are they following you?"

"They weren't. They were following you. Marcel is extremely jealous. They saw us together on the train. They were probably following you all day. They weren't expecting me in the cafe. And I didn't expect them. When I saw them, I panicked and ran."

Ernest nearly believed her. But he had never mentioned Shakespeare and Company to her the night before. If she had lied once, she had undoubtedly lied several times. He was sure most of her story was false. He was about to tell her that when the phone rang again.

Sylvia returned. She served Renata a cup of tea and then answered the phone. "*Oui*. . . . Yes, he is. One moment please. . . . It's for you, Ernest."

He took the phone. "Hello?"

"Hemingway? It's Louis Offenbach." Noise from the other end nearly drowned Offenbach out.

"Where the hell are you?"

"At a party at Caspar Zinadi's. I've got the information you want. And more. Meet me here."

"Where does Zinadi live?"

"On the rue Monge. Number eight. Can you find it?"

"Yeah. It's near my apartment. I'll be there in fifteen minutes."

"Bring your money." Offenbach clicked off.

Ernest grabbed his coat. "Let's go to a party."

Sylvia laughed. "Not me. I've got a night's work ahead of me and it's not going to get done if I go partying."

"What party?" asked Renata.

"It'll be a surprise. Put your coat on and let's move." Ernest blew Sylvia a kiss and opened the door.

"I'm . . . I'm not really in the mood for a party," Renata said.

"Neither am I. But I'm going and so are you."

"What if I say no?"

"Then I'll walk over to the phone and call Inspector Dupré of the Paris police and tell him that you're involved in the theft of my manuscripts and the murder of a German citizen near the Seine." Ernest was bluffing but he had nothing to lose. He watched her carefully to see if she gave anything away. "He was a Nazi, incidentally."

She was good. He had to give her credit for that. Her face registered disbelief, then amusement. "You're joking."

"Suit yourself." He moved toward the telephone.

"All right," she said. "I'll go. But only to make you happy. I have no idea what you're talking about."

"Of course not—I just have a perverse sense of humor."

Renata stubbed out her cigarette and donned her coat. "Thank you, Miss Beach, for your hospitality. I'll come back someday and buy a book."

"Have a good time, wherever you're going," Sylvia said. "Where *are* you dragging Miss Lande, Ernest?"

"Caspar Zinadi's."

"I thought Dada was dead."

"Terminal but lingering." Ernest opened the door. "Thank you, Sylvia."

The rain had stopped. Renata stood under a street lamp, caught in the middle of the pale yellow light like a cabaret performer. "I don't know what a Dada party is," she said.

"You'll love it. There'll be lots of mysterious people there—you'll feel right at home."

This time it was Renata who did not return the smile.

* * *

The worn wipers on the Mercedes streaked the windshield with arcs of dirt. When the rain ended, Kurdorf stepped out and wiped down the windshield with his handkerchief.

The car was parked under a broken street light at the end of the rue de l'Odéon. As Kurdorf cleaned the windshield, he glanced regularly at the bookstore which Hemingway had entered fifteen minutes earlier.

He and Dietrich had been following Hemingway all day, ever since Hemingway's orchestrated escape from the Mercedes. They had lost him only once—when he bolted from the cafe on the Boulevard St. Germain and tore after two men. A delivery truck filled with caged chickens blocked the narrow street and Dietrich had had to back away as Hemingway disappeared.

Anticipating Goering's fury, Kurdorf had feared for his life. When Dietrich suggested that they call Goering and tell him that Hemingway had gotten away, Kurdorf bellowed, ordering Dietrich to drive to the Boulevard St. Michel. The angry, confident way Kurdorf spoke made the Boulevard St. Michel sound like a significant destination, but he had no strategy in mind—it was simply that the Boulevard St.-Michel was the only main thoroughfare he could remember.

It was a lucky memory. The Mercedes skimmed past Hemingway as he leaned against a traffic light along the boulevard. They followed him, first to the police station, then to the river.

At the Seine, Kurdorf told Dietrich to stay in the car while he strolled along the quai. Hemingway and another man—a policeman, probably—joined a knot of people near the water. Kurdorf's eyes were fairly useless beyond forty feet, so he cautiously walked closer until he could see that Hemingway and the others were standing over a body. He hid behind a tree in the shadows. Hemingway and the flics were too interested in the body. No one noticed him.

His heart nearly stopped when he saw the man Hemingway had accompanied from the police station reach into the corpse's coat pocket and take out the party's armband. Instinctively, Kurdorf reached into his side pocket where his own armband was folded neatly.

Fighting an overwhelming urge to run, Kurdorf calmly returned to the Mercedes. He made no attempt to get a closer look at the dead man. He knew it was Schmidt.

He had to tell Goering! He looked in vain for a telephone. Then he saw that Hemingway was walking away from the river.

There was no time for a phone call. He got into the car and ordered Dietrich to follow Hemingway.

They tailed Hemingway from the river to the bookstore on the rue de l'Odéon. Kurdorf found a phone in a corner café and called Goering.

"Yes?"

"It's Kurdorf. Schmidt is dead."

"How do you know?"

"Hemingway went to the police. He and a policeman went to the river. Schmidt's body was there, surrounded by more police."

"Were the documents there?"

"No."

"Where is Hemingway now?"

"In a bookstore on the rue de l'Odéon."

"I'll be there," said Goering and hung up.

That was twenty minutes ago. Kurdorf finished cleaning the windshield and gave another look toward the bookstore. A woman stood before the front door, talking to someone in the shop. Kurdorf waited until she walked into the bookstore, then got back into the Mercedes.

Goering was sitting in the back seat. "Not very observant, are you?"

"I was watching the bookstore," said Kurdorf, startled by Goering's appearance. "I didn't hear you get into the car."

"Is Hemingway still there?"

"Yes."

"Good. Now tell me what happened tonight."

Kurdorf had been rehearsing what he would say to Goering; there were few pauses in his story. When he was done, Goering nodded, then lit a cigarette. "Are you positive there was no suitcase next to Schmidt? No sign of the documents?"

"Nothing," replied Kurdorf. "What do you think happened to Schmidt?"

"We can safely assume that he did not die from natural causes. As for the two men who followed Hemingway from the cafe, they were Russians. Cheka agents. I spoke to Beria this afternoon. They've been following Hemingway since Lausanne."

"Has Beria ordered them off?"

"Not yet. He says he will as soon as they report to him. I don't believe him."

"Why are we following Hemingway?" asked Kurdorf.

"Because he either has the other half of the documents or knows who does and will lead us to them."

"You didn't believe him when he said he knew nothing about the Romanov documents?"

"Not a word."

"And what about Beria?" asked Kurdorf, peering down the empty street. "What else did he say?"

"He agreed to meet me tomorrow morning. I told him we'd recovered the documents and were ready to do business. I'm bringing them to the Denfert-Rochereau at six. We both said we'd come alone. We both lied, naturally."

Kurdorf pulled out his Paris street guide and circled the area around the Denfert-Rochereau, writing "Six A.M." in the margin.

"Why are you doing that?"

"An old accountant's habit." Kurdorf tucked the guide into his jacket pocket. "What do you think the Bolsheviks will do with Anastasia?" Kurdorf imagined her in the dusty underground cell that had been her home for several weeks.

"Nothing."

"I don't understand."

"They'll never have the chance." Goering crossed his arms and looked out the window into the darkened doorway of a *charcuterie*.

"I thought we kidnapped Anastasia in order to sell her to the Bolsheviks."

"Originally, yes. But Hitler and I came up with a variation." For the next five minutes, Goering outlined the plan to offer Anastasia to both the Bolsheviks and the White Russians. Once both sides paid a hundred thousand dollars, Anastasia would be eliminated. The White Russians would be told that the Bolsheviks had killed her.

Kurdorf was appalled. Since Burchardt's murder, he had begun to regret his involvement in the entire operation. And he certainly wanted nothing more to do with violence. "But isn't there a problem," he said.

"Problem?"

"How can you convince both the Bolsheviks and the Whites that she's genuine when there's only one set of documents left?"

"We'll give the Bolsheviks the documents we kept. And we'll recover the rest for the Whites through Hemingway. He must have them or know who does."

"What if we never find them?"

"For your sake, Kurdorf, I wouldn't even consider that possibility."

Kurdorf felt ill. He'd seen Goering kill once. He knew Goering would not hesitate to kill him, either.

Dietrich turned to Goering, his right hand pointing down the street. "It's Hemingway."

Goering looked toward the bookstore. Hemingway and a woman were standing outside. As they started down the rue de l'Odéon, Dietrich shoved the Mercedes into gear.

"Not so fast," warned Goering. "Give them room."

Kurdorf wondered if Hemingway would also be killed. He felt an asthma attack coming on. A coughing spasm racked his body. He wiped his mouth with a soiled handkerchief.

Goering eyed him disgustedly. "Go back to your room. You're not doing me any good here."

Kurdorf did not protest. As soon as he was out of the car, the Mercedes rolled away. He studied his street guide. He had a long walk ahead. That was good. He needed to sort things out.

As he watched the Mercedes vanish into the night, he decided one thing: he would not let Anastasia die.

CHAPTER 18

The walk through the rain-slicked streets of the Latin Quarter was good for Ernest. He cooled down, controlled his anger. Instead of accusing Renata of lying, he spoke understandingly of her problem with her lover. Not that he'd changed his mind about her; she was a liar—he had no doubt about that. But he wanted to play along with her for a while. Somehow, she was involved with his missing manuscripts.

Three blocks from Caspar Zinadi's apartment, she slipped her arm through his, obviously comforted by his solace. He liked walking this way with her, as if they were lovers out for a stroll. He wondered if they would become lovers before the night was out. He wondered just how far she would go to protect her lies.

Turning left on the rue Monge, he guided her to number eight, a stone house fronted by a modest courtyard. The sound of a noisy party blared from the open windows on the first and second floors.

A drunken woman stood in the middle of a crumbling fountain in the courtyard, singing "*La Marseillaise*" as she shed her clothes. A little man wearing a white apron and chef's hat crouched at her feet, catching her chemise before it hit the ground.

"What kind of a party is this?" asked Renata.

"A Dada party."

"What's Dada?"

Ernest almost asked her how she could live in Paris and not know about Dada, particularly if her lover was a painter. But he withheld his question, not wanting to call her bluff.

"Dada is a movement of writers, painters, philosophers, anyone who wants to participate. They think traditional art is meaningless. They have contempt for logic. They champion madness and disorder."

"What do you think of this Dada?"

"Most of it's crap—but then most of everything is crap."

They reached the door. Before Ernest knocked, a tall woman in a black satin gown opened the door. "Dada is dead," she said.

"Rest in peace." Ernest stepped aside for Renata to pass.

"Dada is dead," repeated the woman at the door. "Dead, red, bed, fed."

"At least we know we're in the right place," Ernest said.

The first floor of Zinadi's apartment was one room that ran from the front to the back of the building. The room was packed with revelers, many garbed in strange costumes. The air was thick with cigarette smoke and the smell of too many people jammed into too small a space. The only ones sitting down were three women perched on a spiral staircase that wound up to the second floor. A Negro jazz band played across the room, their music barely audible over the din.

Ernest turned three hundred and sixty degrees, searching for Offenbach. Someone slapped him on the shoulder. "Ernest Hemingway! The *l'enfant terrible* of American prose." It was Caspar Zinadi, the self-proclaimed Prince of Dada. Zinadi was a head shorter and a decade older than Ernest. His hair was prematurely gray and his eyeglasses were nearly as thick as Joyce's.

"Hello, Caspar. How's tricks?"

"Dada is dead."

"So I've heard." Ernest introduced Zinadi to Renata.

"Charmed," said Zinadi.

"What do you mean, Dada is dead?" asked Renata.

"This is Dada's funeral. We bury Dada tonight."

"Where is the dear departed?" Ernest so far had been unable to pick Offenbach out of the crowd.

Zinadi pointed to a pinewood coffin standing on two wooden saw horses in the middle of the room. "Come with me," he said and escorted them to the casket. Inside it were Dada magazines, Dada posters, Dada pamphlets, Dada paintings, Dada photographs, Dada collages, Dada mobiles, Dada newspapers, Dada books, Dada everything.

"What's going to take Dada's place?" asked Renata.

Zinadi shrugged. "Nothing. Isn't that beautiful? What could be purer than nothing?"

"Something will come along," Ernest said.

Zinadi's eyes suddenly widened behind his fishbowl glasses.

"Something already has." He excused himself and approached a sultry-looking blonde who had cut a hole in the middle of her dress and was writing poetry on her bare stomach with a quill pen.

"This is very strange," Renata said.

"You haven't seen anything yet." Ernest took her hand and plunged into the crowd. "Come on—I'm looking for someone."

Ernest aimed for the back corner. A number of odd sights along the way led him to question Dada's demise. He and Renata passed a man wearing a turban and diaper who was stretched out on a bed of nails. They passed a woman strangling a dead duck. They passed an artist painting a picture without paint, stroking a clean brush against the canvas and whistling "*Auprès de ma blonde*." They passed several men and women who were shredding a book of poetry and stuffing the pages into the mouth of a very large, very dead fish; two Americans who were reciting nursery rhymes they had composed in their own incomprehensible language; a man who claimed he had been hypnotized by his cat; two women dressed as dead soldiers, their faces powdered white, their eyes blackened like refugees from the *Cabinet of Dr. Caligari*. They passed more poets, more painters, more writers, more con men, more lunatics.

Finally, they reached the back of the room. Louis Offenbach was busily scribbling notes on his right hand as he interviewed a man clad in a black caftan and carrying a set of golf clubs.

"Who's your friend, Louis?" asked Ernest.

Offenbach said something in German and the golfer glumly trudged off.

Offenbach eyed Renata. "Who's *your* friend, Hemingway?"

"The Kaiser's mother."

"A sense of humor is not your strong point." Offenbach gloved his right hand, then removed the glove to his left. He squinted at his notated palm. "I've got the information you wanted."

Ernest turned to Renata. "Excuse us for a second."

"Don't worry about me—I won't be bored." Standing next to her was a man wearing a crown of thorns and reading aloud from the Bible.

Ernest and Offenbach retreated into a dimly lit alcove under the staircase.

"So who's Beria?" asked Ernest. "Who's Burchardt?"

Offenbach extended his inky palm. "So where's your money?"

Ernest forked over most of Gertrude Stein's cash. Offenbach quickly audited the bills, smiled. "Beria is a Cheka agent. A rising officer. He was called to Paris several weeks ago. I don't know why. Burchardt was a rich industrialist from Berlin, actually outside Berlin. He and his chauffeur were killed three weeks ago."

"Where?"

"About five miles east of Paris."

"Why were they killed?"

"I've heard only rumors."

"I'll listen."

"You'll also pay. My time is valuable."

Ernest surprised Offenbach by handing over more money without an argument. Offenbach didn't count the bills this time. "It's believed that the Grand Duchess Anastasia is still alive and that she was living on Burchardt's estate."

"The daughter of the Czar? The daughter of the Romanov Czar?"

"Top marks. She had some sort of falling out with Burchardt and came to Paris. She ended up in an asylum. Burchardt convinced her to return with him. She was doing exactly that the night Burchardt was killed."

"Where is she now?"

"That would cost you ten times what you've given me—if I knew. And I don't."

"Was she kidnapped by the people who killed Burchardt? You must have heard something."

Offenbach shook his head. "Nothing really. . . ." He paused.

"Come on, Louis—tell me!"

"It will cost you."

"I'm broke. There's nothing left."

"I'll take an IOU—if you don't honor it, I'll show it to everyone in town, let them know you can't be trusted."

"You can trust me."

"All right—give me your IOU."

"Where? On your hand?"

"Don't you have a piece of paper? I thought you were a writer."

Ernest found a pawnbroker's ticket in his wallet—he had hocked his watch five weeks earlier. He borrowed Offenbach's pen to write the IOU on the back of the ticket. "How much?"

"Six hundred francs will do it."

Ernest handed the IOU to Offenbach. "Now tell me what's worth six hundred francs."

"Burchardt came to Paris in his Rolls-Royce. The police know he left the city with Anastasia in it. But the car was never found. I was told tonight that a Rolls bearing a strong resemblance to Burchardt's is parked in the garage in the Montanais."

The Montanais was the most exclusive brothel in Paris. "Why there?"

"That's all I know." Offenbach made a motion to leave. "Thank you for a most profitable evening."

"Hold it." Ernest plunked one hand on Offenbach's shoulder, snatching away the money and the IOU from the German's grasp. "I really appreciate your help, Louis. I'll return the favor some day."

Offenbach's protests were muted by Ernest's right hook, a shot that propelled Offenbach through the crowd and into the Dada-filled coffin. The casket collapsed, burying Offenbach in a downpour of Dada paraphrenalia.

"Rough and tumble—isn't that the way you Americans would describe it?" asked someone from above Ernest's head.

He looked up. Renata was sitting on the tenth step of the staircase, a vantage point from which she could easily have overheard everything Offenbach had told him.

"What the hell are you doing there?" demanded Ernest.

She started down the staircase. "Just resting—all this oddity tires me out."

Like hell, thought Ernest. But the charade had to continue, at least for a while. He was about to utter yet another unctuous comment when a gun was fired on the second floor.

For several seconds, the party stopped—no one moved, no one spoke. Then the man with the golf clubs screamed, triggering a stampede for the the door as people pushed, clawed, climbed over one another in a mad attempt to get out of the apartment. Offenbach, shoving two women out of his way, was the first to escape.

Ernest caught Renata before she fell under a dozen people clamoring down the stairs. He held her against the wall, shielding her with his body. "Are you all right?" His concern was genuine.

"I think so."

He was pressing himself tightly against her, only too aware of the effect her body was having on his. Feeling his response, she moved against him, wrapping her arms around his neck and kissing him passionately.

Returning her kiss, he unbuttoned her coat, his hands gently touching her, her shoulders, her neck, A second gunshot from upstairs jolted them apart.

"This isn't the place for this," she said breathlessly.

The room was deserted, the floor littered with the spilled contents of the casket and discarded bits of costume. "We have to talk," said Ernest.

Renata buttoned her coat. "We can go to my hotel."

"Not now—I have some business to take care of."

Renata kissed him again. "I'm staying at the George V. Room 416," she said and walked out.

Ernest climbed the stairs, his curiosity aroused by the gunshots. He was fairly certain they weren't meant for him, but he had to make sure.

Zinadi stood outside the last of three rooms on the second floor. Ernest looked past him through the open door. A young man with a gun sat on the edge of a large bed.

"What's his problem?"

"I don't know."

"Who is he?"

"His name's Villwahr—Allan Villwahr. He's a painter."

"Friend of yours?"

"Yes."

Villwahr spun the chamber of the gun. Plaster chips speckled the bed. Two large bullet holes splintered the ceiling.

"Why two shots?"

"They were warnings. He wanted people to go away. He says he wants to die alone."

"Why does he want to kill himself?"

"He won't tell me."

Ernest cautiously entered the bedroom. Villwahr aimed the gun at him. "Leave me alone," he said.

Ernest stopped several feet from the bed. "Hello, Allan," he said, looking above. "Nice holes up there. Were you trying to kill the ceiling?"

"The roof. You. Me. It doesn't matter. Nothing matters."

"If it's all the same to you, I'd just as soon live. I still have a few good years in me."

"I don't."

"Not if you put a bullet in your brains. How old are you?"

"Twenty-three."

"So am I."

"Isn't that nice," said Villwahr, raising the gun to Ernest's chest. "Were you in the war?"

"Yeah. You?"

Villwahr smiled. "Do you know why I can't shoot the top of my head off?"

"No."

"Some German bastard beat me to it. The doctors put a steel plate in my head."

Ernest inched closer to the bed. "You're not alone—other guys have the same thing."

"Fuck them and fuck you." Villwahr turned the gun to his face. "The pain never stops. I want it to stop forever."

"I carry around a few souvenirs from the war, too. In my legs."

"Any pain?"

"Sometimes."

"It always hurts with me." Villwahr's finger tightened on the trigger.

"I'm curious about something."

"Leave me alone."

"Come on, Allan. Just a few questions."

Villwahr said nothing.

"Can you still paint?"

"Yes."

"Are you healthy—besides the head pain?"

"Yes."

"What about women? Do you still screw?" Ernest stepped a foot closer.

"Yes."

"Then why the hell do you want to kill yourself?"

Villwahr rested the gun in his lap, but kept a firm grip on the butt. "The pain. There are nights—weeks—when I can't sleep. The doctors give me medicine that does nothing. I lie awake and think about the trenches and the machine guns and the screams. I can hear those screams still. Sometimes I think they will never stop."

"You're alive, Allan. The pain proves that. You can fight it."

Ernest was four feet from Villwahr. He felt sorry for him. He understood the pain. He understood why a man would want to end his own life. But Villwahr was too young. He had reason to live.

The Frenchman smiled again at Ernest. "You're a persuasive fellow but it just doesn't matter." He swallowed half the barrel and pulled the trigger.

Nothing happened.

Ernest jumped onto the bed and jerked the gun from Villwahr's hands. Villwahr struggled for a moment, then fell back onto the bed, curling on his side and crying. Ernest put his hand on Villwahr's shoulder. He could think of nothing to say.

Zinadi knelt beside Villwahr and comforted him. Ernest cracked open the gun's chamber. There were four bullets left. The gun had jammed.

Ernest fiddled with the firing mechanism. "I've got to get going, Caspar."

"Thank you, Ernest."

"Don't thank me—he was going to kill himself. Thank Colt for making at least one pistol that didn't work perfectly." Ernest stuffed the gun in his belt; he didn't trust Villwahr not to repeat his suicide attempt.

Downstairs, the musicians were packing away their instruments. Ernest kicked a book of Dada poetry across the floor. In the courtyard, the man who had been reclining on the bed of nails now stood shivering, his arms crossed across his naked chest. He wore only his diaper and turban.

"You can go back in," said Ernest. "It's safe."

"*Merci, monsieur.* In the excitement I left my coat."

Walking into the street, Ernest tried not to laugh at the absurdity of it all. Maybe Villwahr was right, maybe nothing mattered.

A cab passed and Ernest hailed it. "To the Montanais," he said. "And I'm in a hurry."

"The Montanais! No wonder you're in a hurry."

Ernest was not in the mood for a chat with the cabbie. "I'll give you an extra ten francs if you get me there in ten minutes without saying another word."

The driver stepped on the gas and shut his mouth.

CHAPTER 19

"The papers you want are in Herr Goering's room," the whore whispered into Offenbach's ear. "But they're nothing but a bunch of silly writing by some American named Hemingway."

"How do you know?"

"Because Dietrich—one of Goering's men—told me. And men don't lie when they're in bed with me."

Her name was Greta. *Zaftig*, with light blue eyes and wheat-colored hair, she was one of the most popular whores at the Montanais. She was also one of Offenbach's most reliable sources.

"Is Goering in?"

"No."

"Then take me to his room."

Greta feigned outrage over the demand. "But Herr Offen—"

"Just take me to his room." They were standing alone near the staircase on the Montanais's third floor. Offenbach handed her two hundred francs.

Greta folded the money and dropped it down her abundant cleavage. "All right. But if you're caught—"

"I won't be caught."

"I hope not." she said, starting up the staircase.

Offenbach followed, his eyes looking away from her swaying hips. Such gyrations were wasted on him; he'd never been interested in women.

Reaching the fourth floor, they walked down the corridor to the last door.

"Is this Goering's room?" asked Offenbach.

"Yes."

Offenbach knocked on the door. There was no response. He turned the doorknob. Locked.

"I don't have to give the money back, do I?"

"Leave me alone, Greta," said Offenbach.

The whore gratefully hurried down the hallway and down the stairs.

Offenbach took out his wallet. The only thing he'd learned from his father—a master locksmith—was how to unlock doors. Extracting a thin, jagged wire from his wallet, he knelt down and worked the pick into the lock.

Twenty seconds later, he slipped into Goering's room. He was breathing rapidly. Sweat trickled down his face. The room was pitch-black. Through the thin walls, he heard a whore moaning in theatrical ecstasy from the next room. Phony bitch, he thought as he turned on an overhead light.

The room was small and sparsely furnished; the Montanais's fancier accommodations were on the lower floors. Offenbach methodically searched the room for Hemingway's manuscripts. He found nothing of consequence, not in the cheap bureau next to the bed, not in the ancient armoire, not in Goering's suitcase under the bureau.

Where were the manuscripts?

He'd gone to the Montanais because of Hemingway's questions about Nicholas Burchardt. While Offenbach had told Hemingway about the Rolls-Royce possibly being in the bordello's garage, he did not tell him that several Nazis—rumored to have been involved in Burchardt's murder—were staying at the Montanais.

Their lodging at the Montanais made it easy for Offenbach. While he had no sexual interest in the whores there, he was a frequent visitor to the brothel's first-floor salon. Like some of her customers, Madam Barbara was German, and Offenbach picked up a wealth of gossip at the Montanais. Madam Barbara never bothered him as he flitted about the room, engaging her customers in conversations which often later appeared in the pages of his newspaper. Like everything at the Montanais, Madam Barbara's generosity had a price—Offenbach always had to write glowingly about her and her establishment.

The madam, however, would not be pleased to find out that he had broken into Goering's room. Madam Barbara was sympathetic to the Nazi cause and a great admirer of Goering's war exploits. Because of that, she had provided lodging for Goering and his men.

It was one of those men who had told Greta that Hemingway's

THE HEMINGWAY PAPERS

manuscripts had been stolen from the Gare de Lyon and were now in Goering's room.

But where in Goering's room?

He looked around the depressing scene. Nothing. Absolutely nothing. He paced the room. Passing the bed, his foot brushed against something. He bent down, reached under the bed and drew out a small brown canvas case. The initials EMH were embossed above a tarnished silver latch. Resting the case on the bed, Offenbach opened it and smiled.

The case was filled with manuscripts and blue-covered notebooks, exactly the kind of notebooks he'd seen Hemingway scrawling in while sipping *café au lait* at a restaurant on the Place St.-Michel.

He flipped through the contents of the case. Short stories, poems, even the early chapters of a novel. He'd found a treasure chest.

Quickly, he shoved the notebooks, manuscripts, and carbons under his shirt. What he couldn't fit there, he crushed into his coat pockets. Then he pushed the empty case under the bed and cautiously opened the door. The corridor was deserted.

He slowly approached the stairs. He didn't want any of the manuscripts working free and falling to the floor. He didn't want to explain anything to Madam Barbara or Hermann Goering.

A woman in a clinging green evening gown passed him as he came down the stairs. Offenbach looked the other way. He couldn't wait to be out of the Montanais and in a cab on his way to the Right Bank, where he knew an English writer of little talent but large bank account who would pay handsomely for Hemingway's manuscripts.

Glistening black limousines stood double-parked along the Boulevard Raspail. A dozen chauffeurs huddled in front of the Montanais, smoking cigarettes and exchanging secrets about their distinguished employers. They fell discreetly silent when Ernest passed.

Although Offenbach had told him that Burchardt's Rolls-Royce was in the garage behind the whorehouse, Ernest had decided to check out the action inside the Montanais before sneaking off to the back.

He walked up the half-moon driveway that led to Paris's premier bordello, which years ago had been carved out of two adjacent townhouses. According to local legend, the building on the right had been owned by a notorious gangster. His neighbors on the left were a solemn order of nuns. Not wishing to be associated with the other, each party had sold out to Madam Barbara, who had assured the nuns that she ran a home for wayward girls. Thus was born the Montanais.

A grandfather clock chimed midnight as Ernest swaggered into the lobby. An ornate chandelier sparkled above the dark red carpet. Ernest recognized a top government official, a magistrate renowned for the high moral tone of his decisions, and a famous essayist who published an archly conservative weekly newspaper. Two dour-faced butlers helped the men with their hats and coats, the champagne-sopped magistrate requiring a helping hand to the door.

A string quartet played Beethoven in a large room off the lobby. This was the Montanais's heralded salon, where a man could sip fine wine and appraise the classy whores as they paraded before him. The salon was dark, lit only by candles set along the walls in jeweled sconces. The candles cast an amber glow through the room, creating a warm, intimate atmosphere. The scent of perfume was heady.

Ernest stood near the string quartet. A waiter walked past carrying a tray filled with glasses of wine. "Thanks, pal," said Ernest, helping himself to a glass.

Sipping the wine, Ernest casually eyed the couples seated around the room. The men were middle-aged, elegantly dressed, obviously affluent. The women were young and attractive, all clad in evening gowns that were cut too low to pass anywhere but in a whorehouse. Except for an occasional kiss, their conduct was most decorous. It was upstairs, where a future king of England once dallied regularly with two whores at the same time, where less decorous events occurred.

"May I help you?" asked a woman in her early sixties. A touch of German accented her French. Her evening gown was far from daring, no doubt because her figure was far from lithe. Ernest had heard much about the Montanais and he guessed that this was Madam Barbara.

"I just got into Paris," he said. "I'd like some company for the evening."

She looked dubiously at his threadbare clothes. "Our rates are extremely high—even for a handsome young man like you."

"I know about your prices. They're not a problem. I'm traveling incognito. Money is no object."

"Wonderful!" The woman took Ernest's hand and squeezed. "I'm Madam Barbara."

"And I'm Stephen Daedalus."

"What kind of company are you interested in tonight?"

"I like virgins—they're so hard to find these days."

Madam Barbara laughed. "I'm afraid we haven't had a virgin since the Prince of Wales graced us with his presence."

Ernest made a slight popping sound with his lips, the Gallic version of a shrug.

"Just wait here, Stephen. I'll find you the next best thing." Madam Barbara flounced out of the salon and went up the staircase. Ernest wondered what she considered to be the next best thing to a virgin.

He walked back into the lobby, empty now but for the twinlike butlers standing solemnly at attention at the foot of the stairs. Turning his back to them, he glanced out a long, narrow window next to the front door. He watched a man climbing into the back of a taxi. As the cab pulled away, Ernest recognized the profile of Louis Offenbach.

Offenbach! What the hell was a pansy like Offenbach doing in a place like the Montanais?

Had he come to the brothel to warn Burchardt's killers that Ernest had been asking questions? Had he tipped Ernest's hand, warned them that Ernest would be searching the garage for Burchardt's Rolls-Royce? Ernest had to stop Offenbach to find out.

He rushed out the door and down the driveway. The taxi was already out of sight. Damn it! He stopped at the curb, aware that the gathered chauffeurs were staring at him; very few of the Montanais's customers ever burst out the front door. Ernest pretended he was drunk and weaved down the sidewalk. He heard the chauffeurs laughing. When he looked back, no one was paying any attention to him. He cut down the alley that separated the Montanais from another palatial residence.

The alley was dark and he walked carefully. The ripe smell of garbage filled the air. Ernest barely discerned a mound of trash piled against the building. He remembered the same smell when he was blindfolded and being led by the Nazis out of the Mercedes.

He'd been here before.

With his right hand, he felt along the wall until he touched a doorknob. He remembered stumbling through a door and smelling perfume and cigarettes. He remembered he'd heard women laughing.

This was where the Nazis had taken him, he was sure of it. The stairs he'd gone down had led to the basement or some kind of cavern under the Montanais.

He tried the door. Locked.

A cat suddenly leaped out of the garbage, spitting at him as it passed. Momentarily startled, Ernest shook his head at his own fear, then proceeded down the alley. He had no trouble finding the garage, even in the darkness. Large enough to house at least six cars, the garage dominated the area behind the bordello. He opened a side door and walked in.

The garage smelled of gasoline, its concrete floor marbled with dark oil stains. Only one car, sheathed by a tarpaulin, was parked inside.

Ernest pulled off the cover. The car was a gray Rolls-Royce; save for a shattered window on the driver's side, it was even more opulent than the limousines outside the Montanais. He opened the back door and sat on the thick leather seat. A portable bar was built into the door under the window. He picked up a samovar emblazoned with the initials "NB."

Nicholas Burchardt, thought Ernest. Offenbach had been right; Burchardt's killers *had* brought the Rolls back with them. Ernest had already concluded that the Nazis were somehow connected to the Montanais; clearly they had killed Burchardt and kidnapped Anastasia, or whoever it was claiming to be a Romanov.

Ernest didn't give a damn about phony Russian princesses, or whatever the hell she was supposed to be.

All he cared about were his manuscripts. He knew the Nazis had them. They were probably somewhere in the Montanais.

The trick was getting them back.

* * *

Anastasia's cell door was locked, so Kurdorf stared at her through the peephole. The guard, a sullen young man named Rheinhardt, stood nearby, the key to the cell dangling on a chain from his belt. Rheinhardt was big and muscular. There was no way Kurdorf could overpower him and free Anastasia.

Kurdorf felt genuinely sorry for her, almost as sorry as he felt for himself. She had eaten little in her weeks of imprisonment. Her face was thinner, her complexion sallow. She rarely got off the lumpy, straw-filled cot. Everytime Kurdorf checked on her, she was staring straight ahead, her eyes glazed and unblinking. Only her shallow breathing betrayed any sign of life.

Kurdorf frowned. Now more than ever he regretted joining the National Socialists. So many people killed: Burchardt, the chauffeur, Bruno Schmidt. Anastasia would be next, unless something was done.

But what could he do?

He was an accountant, not a secret agent. What could he possibly do to save her?

Rheinhardt walked across the dusty corridor and picked up his rifle. Kurdorf shuddered, recalling how he had been in the Mercedes when the car came across the German-French border, a cache of weapons hidden under the back seat; he'd helped smuggle arms. And he was an accomplice to Burchardt's murder. It had to stop.

It had to.

Patting Rheinhardt on the back, Kurdorf decided to go upstairs, perhaps to take a walk around the block. Or perhaps to find the courage to go to the nearest police station and report everything that had happened.

Ernest was coming up the alley when Glasses—one of the Nazis who'd kidnapped him—emerged from the side door. Ernest waited to make sure Glasses, who was walking toward the street, was alone. Then he sank his left hand into Glasses's shoulder, twisted him around and slammed him against the wall. Ernest wedged his forearm against the German's throat, cutting off his scream.

Ernest had thought of threatening the Nazi with the gun he'd taken from Villwahr. But he could tell from the expression of fear on Glasses's face that no such display was needed. "I'm going to let you talk. But if you cry out, I'll break your neck. Understand?"

Glasses nodded and Ernest released him. "You . . . you frightened me," said Glasses, bending over and sucking in several deep breaths.

"Where are the manuscripts?"

Glasses straightened up but said nothing.

Ernest slapped the German's face, knocking off his glasses. "Where are they?"

"Goering has them." The German stooped to retrieve his glasses. Ernest pushed him back against the wall before he could reach them.

"Who's Goering?"

"You've never heard of Hermann Goering?" Kurdorf asked incredulously.

"Was he the guy wearing the long leather coat today?"

"Yes."

"And who the hell are you?"

"My name is Wilhelm Kurdorf."

"All right, Willie, I want the manuscripts back. Can you get them?"

"They're in Goering's room," said Kurdorf, the look of fear returning to his face. "My God! Goering was following you—he must be here!"

"No one followed me," said Ernest, not completely sure that was true. "What about the manuscripts?"

"I can probably get them. But not now. I'll have to wait, make sure Goering is somewhere else."

"The hell with Goering," said Ernest, seething. "I want those manuscripts back now."

"I can't—it's too risky," said Kurdorf. "He may be back here. You have to wait. Goering plans to exchange the Romanov papers this morning."

"The documents he thinks I have?"

Kurdorf nodded. "Some of the Romanov papers were stolen. He thinks you have them."

"Why?"

THE HEMINGWAY PAPERS

A car's headlights suddenly broke the darkness of the alley. "It's Goering!" said Kurdorf, shielding his eyes from the blinding light.

But the car backed out and turned onto the Boulevard Raspail. "How did I get mixed up in this?" demanded Ernest.

"The Bolsheviks said they took your bag by mistake. Goering didn't believe them. He thinks you're involved. He thinks you either have the papers or will lead us to the people who do."

A sudden realization dawned on Ernest: his escape from the Mercedes had been planned. "What happens to Anastasia?"

A look of shock crossed Kurdorf's face. He said nothing. Ernest held the gun he'd taken from Villwahr and shoved it against Kurdorf's forehead. "You can answer my question or I can blow your fucking brains out. Decide."

"All right," said Kurdorf, his voice cracking with fear. "Anastasia is to be sold to both the Bolsheviks and the White Russians. Goering plans to murder her after both sides have paid for her. He's going to blame the Bolsheviks for her death."

"Where do the documents fit in?"

"They prove who she is. Goering originally planned to sell half the documents to the Bolsheviks and half to the Whites. He still wants to do that. He's convinced he'll recover the missing documents through you."

"He's wrong," said Ernest, lowering the gun.

Kurdorf leaned down to pick up his glasses. "I need your help," he said.

Ernest dug his hands into Kurdorf's throat. "We're not partners."

"Goering will kill Anastasia. He'll kill us all. You've got to help."

Ernest took his hands from the German's throat. "Get my manuscripts back and I'll think about it."

"I'll try."

"I want them tonight."

"All right," said Kurdorf. "Where do I bring them?"

"There's a café near here called the Dome. It's on the Boulevard Montparnasse. I'll be there at three. That gives you almost three hours. If you're not there, you're a dead man."

"I'll be there," said Kurdorf.

Ernest wondered if he should try getting the manuscripts back himself. But he didn't know where Goering's room was. And Goering might have followed him to the Montanais. Only a damn fool would go up against Goering and his men alone. "Remember," said Ernest. "The Dome at three."

Kurdorf watched Hemingway go down the alley and hail a cab. He waited until Hemingway was gone, then opened the side door of the Montanais. A man was standing in the shadows. Kurdorf had never been more frightened in his life. He reached out and steadied himself against the door frame.

"Come now, Herr Kurdorf," said Goering. "Pull yourself together. What would your friend Hemingway think?"

CHAPTER 20

Ernest walked into the elegant lobby of the George V. As he approached the central staircase, he returned the desk clerk's haughty gaze, adding just the proper expression of disdain to force the clerk to look away. He walked up the stairs unchallenged.

A chambermaid smiled at him as he padded down the corridor to Renata's suite. He knocked twice.

"Yes?"

"It's Hemingway."

The door opened. She was hastily pulling a satin robe over a filmy blue negligee. "Come in—I was worried about you."

"You really go first class," Ernest said as he looked around the sitting room. He walked into the bedroom and checked the bathroom, making sure they were alone.

"You sound as though you disapprove," Renata said when he returned to the front room.

"It's a little precious for my taste."

"You get used to it." She settled on the couch, tucking her legs under her.

"Got anything to drink?" asked Ernest, shucking off his coat.

She shook her head. "I can call room service."

"Don't bother." He sat next to her on the couch. Her robe had parted. The bodice of her negligee was cut low.

"Did you find anything at the Montanais?" she asked, confirming Ernest's suspicion that she'd overheard his conversation with Offenbach.

He deliberately countered with a question of his own. "What were you doing on the *Orient Express* last night?"

"I told you—I was returning to Paris. My lover and I—"

"Cut the crap—you're not good at it. You said before that I had talked about Shakespeare and Company. I hadn't. You claimed you lived in Paris with an artist, yet you're staying in the George V. You've never heard about the Dada movement. You're a con and I'm the sap who's getting suckered."

"That's not true, Ern—"

"What do you know about Nicholas Burchardt?"

That got to her. She stood and started searching for a cigarette, not answering until she found one in her purse, lit it and took a long drag. "My real name is Renata Burchardt," she said. "Nicholas Burchardt was my father."

Ernest had been right—she *had* been lying to him.

Renata turned toward him, her robe parting even further. He wasn't sure if she was deliberately doing it. And it really made no difference: he'd never wanted a woman more than he wanted her.

"If I tell you everything," she said, "you have to promise to tell me what you learned at the Montanais."

"If I think you're leveling with me, I may help you. But no promises."

"All right." She stubbed out her cigarette and lit another. She returned to the couch. She did not close her robe. Her nipples were clearly outlined under the silk of her negligee. "Three years ago my father met two Russian refugees in Berlin. Since he was born in Russia, he felt great sympathy for them. He offered to help them. They came to live with my family—it was not the first time he'd brought home strays. Several of our servants are Russian. But these two were different. Or I should say, the woman was different."

"Was she the Grand Duchess Anastasia?"

"You know a great deal, don't you?" she asked, her hand brushing against his thigh, lingering, then moving away.

"Was it Anastasia?"

"Yes. We didn't believe it at first. But she had documents with her and she was extremely well educated. She spoke several languages and knew everything about the Romanovs."

"What happened?"

"She was not well. She'd been through a terrible ordeal, an ordeal that had taken its toll on her. She became depressed, suspicious. She left our home several months ago."

"To come to Paris?"

"Yes. My father hired detectives to find her. They did—in

an institution in Montmartre. She had tired to kill herself and failed. As far as the French were concerned, she was insane, a diagnosis that they considered confirmed when she started telling them who she was."

"Did anyone believe her?"

"Would you?"

"No."

"Neither did they. My father made many trips to Paris to see her. Eventually she agreed to return to Germany. He was bringing her back when he and his chauffeur were killed and Anastasia was kidnapped." Renata began to cry.

Ernest fought the urge to comfort her. He needed answers, not tears. "Do you know who killed your father?" asked Ernest, suspecting the answer.

She dried her eyes with the sleeve of her robe. "We believe it was a group called the National Socialist party. There is a man named Goering, Hermann Goering. He was a famous pilot in the war. He's in Paris. The day before yesterday, one of his men tried to deliver some of Anastasia's documents to the Bolsheviks in the Gare de Lyon. We intercepted him."

"We?"

"The young man who saved Anastasia and helped her flee Russia is with me. He's staying in a room down the hall. His name is Sergei. He's traveling as my brother. He was even wearing a Star of David as part of the charade." She leaned forward, her hand moving across her neck.

"Why the games?"

"Sergei is a marked man. The Cheka has put a price on his head for helping Anastasia escape."

"Did he kill the Nazi courier?"

"He'd kill them all for Anastasia."

"I still want to know why you were on the *Orient Express*." Ernest glanced at her full breasts straining against the negligee.

"Only half the documents were in the case the Nazi courier was carrying. Sergei went to the Gare de Lyon, hoping to spot the Bolshevik agent who was waiting to receive the documents. What Sergei saw was your wife, frantically looking for a small suitcase similar to the one he'd just taken from the Nazi. Sergei suspected that your wife was a Bolshevik agent."

Ernest laughed. "Hadley! She's as American as Warren Harding."

"So are a lot of Bolshevik sympathizers," said Renata. "Sergei found out your wife's name and destination and I took the same train to Lausanne. I followed the two of you to your hotel, then I followed you onto the *Orient Express*. I had to find out who you really were, what you knew, why you were going to Paris."

"I had nothing to do with Anastasia or her documents. And I'm certainly not an agent for Mother Russia."

"I know that now. . . ." Renata began again to cry. "Oh, damn, Ernest. I'm so sorry. I'm so sorry for everything." She reached across and held his hand.

Ernest believed her. "Everything will work out," he said, uncomfortably aware that he was echoing a similar prediction he'd made to Hadley. He put his arms around Renata.

She stopped sobbing and rested her head against his chest. He stroked her hair. She raised her head and he kissed her. Her hands caressed his face. She reached behind him and turned off the lamp, plunging the room into darkness. "It's better this way," she said, slipping off her robe and putting his hand on her breast. Her tongue worked madly against his. He lowered the straps of her negligee and cupped her breasts. She unbuttoned his shirt, bending to gently kiss his chest. He picked her up and carried her into the bedroom.

Hermann Goering sat in the single chair in his room at the Montanais, drinking brandy and weighing his options.

Something had to be done with Kurdorf. Kurdorf, who was being kept in the cell next to Anastasia, was a traitor and traitors had to be punished. Severely punished.

But Goering faced a more serious problem: what was he going to do with Anastasia?

If Hemingway knew about her, how many others also knew? Goering had overheard Hemingway claim to Kurdorf that he was an innocent bystander, that he had nothing to do with the theft of the Romanov documents. Goering didn't believe him. Goering did not kill Hemingway in the alley outside the Montanais because he was certain Hemingway would still lead him to the missing documents.

Time, however, was running out. Goering decided that he—not Kurdorf—would keep the appointment with Hemingway. He would make the American an offer: Hemingway's manuscripts in return for the missing papers. If Hemingway still refused, then most assuredly he was an innocent. And he would die, for Goering could not afford any outsider—particularly a journalist—to know about their plans.

Goering, of course, no longer had Hemingway's manuscripts. He'd discovered minutes earlier that someone had stolen them from the case under his bed. He immediately suspected Kurdorf. But Kurdorf had denied taking them. Goering believed him—if Kurdorf had the manuscripts, he would have given them to Hemingway in the alley.

Goering wasn't interested in the thief who stole the manuscripts. What was vital was that Hemingway still thought Goering had them, giving Goering an advantage with which to negotiate.

Goering's other valuable tool—half of the Romanov documents—rested on the table next to the bed. Finishing his brandy, he stood and walked to the table.

He had had the foresight to store the Romanov documents in the Montanais's safe. Before coming up to his room, he'd removed them from the safe, preparing for his meeting with Beria at dawn.

Goering picked up Hemingway's empty suitcase. Placing it on the bed, he carefully packed the battered canvas case with the Romanov documents. As he did, he smiled; the idea of using Hemingway's case amused him.

When he had finished, he looked at his watch. Two o'clock. Pouring some more brandy, he contemplated his meeting with Hemingway in sixty minutes.

Ernest awoke in darkness and reached across the bed for Renata. He touched only a bundle of sheets. Then he noticed a red dot of light across the room; Renata was sitting in a chair near the window, smoking a cigarette. Ernest moved across the bed to switch on a lamp.

"Please don't," said Renata, standing and walking naked to the bed. "Sometimes I prefer the dark."

Ernest reached up and gently pulled her down next to

him. His hands moved down her body. She moaned, returning his caresses. They began to make love, more slowly this time. Ernest kissed her neck, her breasts.

Suddenly, he remembered his appointment with Kurdorf.

"Christ," he said. "What time is it?"

"About two-thirty," she said, stroking him.

Ernest reluctantly turned away.

"Is anything wrong?" she asked.

"Nothing—except I have to meet a man named Kurdorf at three."

"The name means nothing to me."

"He's a Nazi. He works with Goering."

"Why are you meeting him?"

Ernest got out of bed, taking a moment to find his clothes strewn on the floor. As he dressed, he told her of his discovery of her father's Rolls-Royce in the garage behind the Montanais and his chance encounter with Kurdorf.

"Kurdorf is supposed to bring my manuscripts," Ernest said as he buttoned his shirt. "I'm meeting him at a cafe called the Dome."

"Let me come with you."

Ernest sat on the edge of the bed. His eyes had grown accustomed to the darkness and he could faintly make out Renata's head resting on the pillow. "Let Sergei and me go with you," she said.

"I have to do this alone. Kurdorf is a frightened man. If he sees anyone else he'll panic and run and I'll never see my manuscripts and you'll never see Anastasia."

"Anastasia? Does that mean you'll help us?"

"In my own way. I'll tell Kurdorf that I know people who want to rescue Anastasia. I'll arrange a meeting. I don't want to see Anastasia die."

Renata put her arms around his neck. "Thank you," she said, kissing him passionately.

Ernest didn't want to leave, but he forced himself to break away from her. "I'll be back," he said and walked out of the bedroom and the suite.

A minute passed. Then Renata turned on the light, went to the telephone and called Sergei.

* * *

The Dome was nearly empty.

Ernest took a table in the corner with a view of the Boulevard Montparnasse. He could see across the street to a long, narrow island in the middle of the Boulevard Raspail, which met Montparnasse in front of the cafe. The statue of some obscure French hero stood on a marble block on the island, his sword raised defiantly toward the sky.

Ernest ordered a *café au lait* and watched the waiter work the gleaming silver coffee machine at the end of the bar. Ernest was partial to the Dome. He liked the comfortable green banquettes and the dark mahogany paneling. Pink-tinted lampshades cut the glare and were easy on the eyes, a plus if you were nursing a hangover. The food was passable and the waiters didn't bother you if you had two hours to kill but only enough francs for a single *croissant*.

Topping the coffee with hot, steaming milk, the waiter served Ernest, who sipped the brew appreciatively. He noticed the cup shaking in his hand. His nerves were on edge. It was Renata: she had really gotten to him. A confusing mix of guilt and desire filled him. He felt guilty because he'd betrayed Hadley. But he also felt desire because he wanted Renata again, wanted to keep seeing her. He had been overwhelmed by her sensuality, by her whole being. He needed her again. And he would have her.

"Good evening, Herr Hemingway."

Ernest had been so lost in his thoughts that he hadn't noticed the man standing next to him come in. It was Hermann Goering.

"Where's Kurdorf?"

"He took violently ill." As Goering sat down, he unbuttoned his coat, then rested his hands on the table. "I'm not armed."

Ernest nodded toward the Boulevard Montparnasse. "But I bet your friends are."

"I came alone."

"Sure," said Ernest, shaking his head as the waiter approached the table.

"I'd like to make a deal with you," said Goering.

Ernest sipped his coffee, then dropped his right hand to his side. "What have you got in mind?"

"A simple exchange—your manuscripts for the Romanov documents."

Ernest sighed. "I don't have them."

"I expected you to say that. But I think you know who does. All you have to do is tell me who has them and you'll get your manuscripts back."

Remembering all the work that had gone into those stories, Ernest was tempted for an instant to tell Goering about Renata Burchardt. But the moment passed, and with it all thoughts of betrayal. "I don't know anything about your Romanov papers."

Goering stared at him. "Did you come here alone?"

"Yes." Ernest inched the gun out of his pocket.

Goering looked around the cafe. Only the bartender and waiter remained. "I believe you," said Goering. "You really don't have the documents. And you don't know who does."

"I'm so relieved."

Goering started to get up. "Good evening, Herr—"

"Sit down, asshole."

"What?"

"I have a gun pointing at your crotch. If you have any affection for your balls, sit down."

Goering hesitated, then obeyed. "I came here in good faith," he said.

"Bullshit. You're here because you somehow found out Kurdorf was going to sell you down the river and you wanted to find out once and for all if I could get you the Romanov documents."

"And you can't."

"But you can get me my manuscripts. And you can get them now."

"I don't have them anymore."

Ernest smashed the barrel of the gun against Goering's knee. Goering winced. "This is a .38 caliber revolver. One shot and you can say goodbye to any plans for descendants."

"Your manuscripts were stolen. I don't know who has them."

Ernest thumbed back the hammer of the .38 so Goering could hear the familiar snapping sound. "I saw guys in the war who lived after their vitals were blown off. They didn't want to live. But they did."

"I tell you I don't—"

"I want the manuscripts."

Goering tried to stop his hands from shaking. "All right. You'll have them. But you'll have to come with me."

"You didn't come alone," said Ernest. "How many men do you have out there?"

Goering didn't answer.

Ernest prodded Goering's knee with the gun. "How many?"

"Two. They're in the car. It's parked on the Boulevard Raspail."

Ernest glanced out the window. There were no cars to be seen. "How far down the block?" asked Ernest, dropping some francs on the table.

"Nearly at the end. They can't see us."

"We're going to go outside and walk the other way down Montparnasse. We're going to find a cab and go to where you've stashed my manuscripts. If your men follow, I'll kill you."

"I understand."

"Good. Let's go." They stood and Ernest pushed Goering out of the cafe.

The street was empty: no cars, no people. The only sound came from the click of the traffic signal changing colors at the corner. They turned left, away from the Boulevard Raspail. It was colder now, the wind sharper.

They had almost reached the corner of Montparnasse and the rue du Depart when Ernest heard a car swerve around the corner on two wheels and roar towards them. "Keep walking," he told Goering, risking a look over his shoulder to see if it was the Mercedes.

It was. And it was only thirty yards away.

Ernest shoved Goering forward, then swiveled around, holding the gun outstretched in both hands, waiting several seconds to draw a line on the driver, then pulling the trigger.

For the second time that night, the gun jammed.

Someone in the Mercedes fired, missing Ernest but shattering the shop window behind him. As Ernest dove to the sidewalk, Goering leaped onto the Mercedes's running board and the car sped out of sight down the Boulevard Montparnasse.

"Goddamn it!" shouted Ernest as he picked himself up and pocketed the useless revolver.

The street was once more quiet and empty.

Cursing his bad luck, Ernest approached the Dome. He

was about to walk in when Renata called to him from across the street.

She was standing in front of the Café Rotonde. Ernest started across Montparnasse. She was wearing a mink coat, the one she'd worn in the Lausanne train station. "What the hell are you doing here?" he demanded.

She took his hands in hers. "I had to—"

Renata's words were lost as the windshield of a nearby car exploded. "Get inside," said Ernest, pushing her into the Rotonde. Hearing another shot, he tumbled to the ground. He spotted the Mercedes down the street. The goddamn Germans were back.

A piece of curb split away. He crawled behind the rear tire of a car. Four more shots rang out. The tire was destroyed. As air whistled from the puncture and the car began to list, he rolled behind the front tire. A flash from a doorway across the street and a bullet ripped through the car's hood, ricocheting through the engine.

Ernest kept his eyes on the doorway. Nothing. Then two more shots erupted, not from the doorway, chipping away the cobblestone near his hand. There was a second gunman up the block, about forty yards from Ernest.

They had him pinned in a crossfire.

Ernest sprang up and sprinted toward the concrete island in the middle of Raspail, diving for cover behind the base of the pedestal.

Ernest saw the Mercedes slowly moving up the boulevard on the other side of the island. The gunmen emerged from the shadows and advanced, keeping him trapped with a steady volley of shots.

Then, suddenly, there was silence.

Ernest peered around the corner of the pedestal. The men had closed ranks and were now only fifty feet away. Methodically, like marksmen at target practice, they loaded their pistols.

The Mercedes was right behind them, ready to whisk them away after they were finished with Ernest.

His only chance was to tear back across Raspail and get into the Rotonde. He brought his knees up, ready to go. He heard the men shoving fresh clips into their guns. He breathed deeply and came out of his crouch.

What he saw when he turned made him freeze.

A third gunman was standing behind the car with the shattered windshield, his pistol raised, his eyes squinting as he aimed and fired off three quick rounds.

Ernest fell to the ground. He heard one of the men behind him cry out, saw the man double over and stagger back to the sidewalk, where he collapsed.

The Mercedes spurted ahead, then stopped, cutting off Ernest's view. There were no more shots. Goering yelled an order in German and the Mercedes bounced on its springs as the wounded man was carried into the car. A scream of agony filled the air. As the Mercedes took off, a body was thrown from the front seat.

Ernest stood, brushing dirt from his clothes. Renata was standing next to the man with gun.

"This must be Sergei," said Ernest.

Renata nodded. "I knew we should have gone with you."

"I'm glad you showed up."

Sergei put his gun away. Renata pointed to the body across the street. "Who's that?"

"I bet it's Kurdorf," said Ernest. "Goering somehow found out that he was going to help me."

They walked to the body. Kurdorf's throat had been cut. Blood streamed down the inclined gutter and into a sewer.

Lights were going on in apartments overhead. People were emerging from the Rotonde to see what had happened.

"We better go," said Renata.

"In a second." Ernest went through Kurdorf's pockets, finding only a dog-eared Paris street guide.

"Our car's around the corner," said Renata.

Ernest dropped the street guide into his own pocket. The crowd was growing. The police were bound to be on their way. "All right," Ernest said and followed Renata and Sergei to their car.

CHAPTER 21

The car was a late model Austin. Sergei drove with Renata at his side. Ernest sat in the back, combing the pages of the street guide he'd found on Kurdorf.

"How do we get to the Montanais?" asked Renata.

"Forget the Montanais."

"But it's got to be where they have Anastasia. And where they have your manuscripts."

"It's also where Goering has his men. They're armed and they don't hesitate to shoot. We'd be damn fools to go rushing in there."

"What do you propose we do?"

Ernest offered no answer. As he continued to skim the street guide, Renata spoke to Sergei in German. They were coasting up the Boulevard Saint-Michel, the Sorbonne on their right.

"Doesn't he speak English?" asked Ernest.

"Only German and Russian. How many languages have you mastered?" snapped Renata.

"I didn't mean it like that. I just wanted to know in case I had to tell him something in a hurry." Ernest sensed a change in Renata. This wasn't the same woman who'd shared her bed with him only an hour earlier. Now she was cold, businesslike. He wondered about her relationship with Sergei, wondered if he, too, was her lover. The thought troubled him, made him jealous

"I'll translate for you," said Renata. "Is there anything in that book?"

"There's not enough light," said Ernest. "Tell him to stop for a second under a street lamp."

Sergei drove three more blocks before finding a suitable spot. Ernest methodically went through the guide book.

The rain that had been falling in spurts all day was turning to snow. Sergei flipped on the windshield wipers as a fine powder dusted the street.

"Here's something," said Ernest. "It's the only thing in the book."

Renata turned excitedly. "What is it?"

"Our friend Kurdorf had circled an area called the Denfert-Rochereau in the fourteenth arrondissement. And he's written 'Six A.M.' in the margin."

"Which means what?"

"Kurdorf said Goering had an appointment this morning with the Bolsheviks. This could be the time and place of that meeting."

Renata lit a cigarette. "Or it could be a meaningless note written years ago by some tourist—that book doesn't look terribly new."

"The Denfert-Rochereau isn't a tourist attraction. No Eiffel Tower. No Sacré-Coeur. No Louvre. It's just a bourgeois neighborhood of no particular distinction. Tourists don't go there, especially not at the crack of dawn."

Renata gazed thoughtfully out her side window. Ernest checked the rest of the book to see if there were any other markings. There weren't. Renata rolled down the window and flicked her cigarette into the snow. "I don't know," she said. "I just don't know."

"You don't have a choice for now—we've got to go there and wait," said Ernest. "You can't storm the Montanais. You'd never get past the front door. The only other alternative is to go to the police."

Renata glared at him. "The police are not to become involved."

Ernest pocketed the street guide. "Why not?"

"They would never believe that the daughter of the Czar was still alive or that she was the victim of a vicious kidnapping. They'd think we were insane. And they just might link Sergei with the killing of the Nazi courier."

"All right," said Ernest, "do what the hell you want to do. Me—I'm going to be at the Denfert-Rochereau at six. I still have a score to settle with this Goering bastard."

It was getting cold in the car. Sergei peeled off his right glove and used it to wipe frost from the inside of the windshield. Ernest crossed his arms and stomped his feet against the floorboard.

"You win, Ernest," said Renata. "Tell us how to get to this Denfert-Rochereau."

Someone was poking him in the ribs. "Wake up—it's almost six."

He'd been dreaming of a shimmering blue lake in Michigan where the fish ran so big that you had to pack two frying pans to cook just one. Renata had been in the dream, swimming naked, beckoning him to join her. He was about to do just that when the poking began. "It's time, Ernest. Wake up!"

Reluctantly, he opened his eyes. Renata was leaning over the front seat. "I'm okay," said Ernest, stretched out along the back seat of the Austin.

"I thought you were dead," joked Renata.

Ernest smiled. "Just dead to the world. Anything happening?"

"See for yourself."

Ernest propped himself up. Snow had fallen heavily during the hour he'd been asleep. It was still dark out; Ernest looked up at a street lamp—snow whipped by wind swirled in the light. Ernest cranked down the window and peered out onto the rue du St. Jacques.

The muffled silence was eerie. The thick blanket of snow was smooth, unmarked by either footsteps or tire treads.

"No one's come down this street," said Ernest.

"Not a soul," said Renata. "And it's already twenty to six."

Ernest buttoned up his coat. "I'm going to do a little reconnoitering. Should be back in five minutes."

Renata said nothing as Ernest climbed out of the Austin and started down the street, the snow crunching under his shoes. He passed no one as he crossed the Boulevard Arago. The empty streets struck him as strange, even for such a rotten morning as this. Then he remembered that it was Sunday and he understood: even the most fanatical churchgoer would wait for a later Mass rather than brave such a storm.

He cut down the rue Leclerc, stopping at a boulevard

whose name he did not know. Taking shelter in the doorway of a well-kept *pension*, he looked down the street. He thought he saw a car parked near the statue of a lion in the middle of the Place Denfert-Rochereau. But the blinding snow made it impossible for him to be sure.

He kept going, nearly slipping on a patch of ice as he crossed the Avenue René Coty. He stopped behind a kiosk near the entrance to a metro station. A church bell echoed across the boulevards.

Ernest chanced a look across the plaza. A car *was* parked near the statue. It wasn't Goering's Mercedes. There appeared to be only one occupant, a man.

Suddenly, a hand gripped Ernest by the leg. He whirled, his own hands knotting into fists, ready to strike. But it was only a small child, an altar boy with his red and white cassock slung over his arm.

"Are you lost?" asked the boy.

Ernest, his heart beating wildly, shook his head.

"The church is warm," said the child, pointing down the block. "We don't get many on a day like this. Why don't you come with me to Mass?"

The boy was standing in the open. Even in a storm like this, the man in the car was bound to notice him. "It's all right," said Ernest.

"Father Broussard will see that you get a warm meal and a place to stay."

Christ, thought Ernest, the little do-gooder thinks I'm a *clochard*, a bum. "Really, you don't have to—"

The boy reached for Ernest's hand. "Come. Father Brou—"

"Listen, boy—I've sinned so much and so long that I have a room reserved in hell. Leave me in peace."

The boy looked pained, as if for the first time his zealousness had failed. Sadly shaking his head, he started off toward the church.

Ernest glanced across the plaza. The door of the car was opening. He must have seen the boy, thought Ernest, watching apprehensively. The man got out, walked to the front of the car and began to brush snow from the windshield. Ernest relaxed; he hadn't been seen. He kept his eyes on the man. As the man was about to get back into the car, he nodded faintly toward a small park across the plaza on the rue Froidevaux.

Ernest followed the man's gaze. There, barely visible behind a row of hedges, stood two men, one tall, the other much shorter. Although he couldn't see their faces, Ernest knew immediately they were the two men who'd attacked him on the quai. Bolsheviks, he reasoned, just like the man in the car—the man Ernest now pegged for Beria, the Cheka agent.

Retracing his steps, Ernest returned to the Austin. As he warmed himself in the back seat, he told Renata and Sergei what he'd seen. When he finished, Sergei spoke to Renata in German.

"He wants to go there immediately, eliminate the Bolsheviks and wait for the Nazis," said Renata.

"Then he can go by himself. We're not the goddamn Marines."

Renata translated for Sergei, who responded angrily. "He has his doubts about your courage."

"I'll be happy to oblige him any day, his choice of weapons," said Ernest. "Tell him I'm not a fool and I don't want to die. Tell him I have a plan."

Renata translated Ernest's statement. Sergei curtly nodded his head. "Ask him to turn off the headlights and slowly drive down this street," said Ernest.

The snow was letting up. At the Boulevard Arago, Ernest ordered Sergei to stop. Then he got out of the car and cautiously looked around the corner of the *pension* towards the Denfert-Rochereau.

A second car had parked in the plaza, across the boulevard from Beria. Too far away to make a positive identification, Ernest was certain it was the Mercedes.

Ernest figured that both Goering and Beria had agreed to meet alone but that neither one would honor that agreement. He'd already seen Beria's men. Goering's troops, he bet, were hidden somewhere in the area behind the Mercedes.

A man climbed out of the Mercedes, carrying a small suitcase. It had to be Goering, about to walk across the plaza to show Beria the Romanov papers.

Ernest returned to the Austin. "Tell Sergei I need his gun," he said as he sat in the back.

Sergei reluctantly handed Ernest his Smith & Wesson. Ernest spun the chamber to check that it was loaded, then released the safety. "I want him to make a right and then hit the gas. We're going to give our friends a little surprise."

Nodding as Renata translated, Sergei jerked the car into gear and pointed the Austin down the Boulevard Arago. Ernest rolled down his window. The storm was over. Sergei floored the gas pedal and the car sped down the snowy street.

Ernest looked through the windshield. About fifty yards ahead, Goering was approaching Beria, walking slowly across the plaza. Both men heard the car at the same moment, both turned to look down the street as the Austin bore down on them.

Ernest braced himself against the back door and stuck the gun out the window. Waiting until the Austin was directly between Goering and Beria, Ernest pumped off three rounds into the air.

The Austin jackknifed on some ice, but Sergei deftly straightened it out, flashing through the plaza and up the Boulevard Raspail.

Through the Austin's rear window, Ernest saw Beria scurry behind his car as Goering, suitcase still clutched in his hand, fell on the ice, trapped in a crossfire as the Bolsheviks and Nazis opened up on each other.

They'd gone too fast through the plaza for Ernest to be positive, but the suitcase in Goering's hand looked a lot like his bag, the one stolen from the Gare de Lyon. He had to get a closer look.

Behind them, gunshots cracked through the plaza.

Ernest's hunch had paid off: since there was mutual distrust between Beria and Goering, each had decided that the Austin belonged to the other side. There would be no exchange of the Romanov documents this morning.

Sergei braked and the car slid to a halt. Ernest dropped the gun on the front seat and opened the door.

"Where are you going?" demanded Renata.

"After Goering. He still has something of mine."

"Let Sergei go with you."

"No. I want you both at the Montanais. It's straight ahead on Raspail near the rue de Vaugirad. It's a big building with a half-moon driveway. If Goering slips through my fingers, someone has to be waiting to make sure he doesn't get away for good." Ernest handed Sergei his gun.

Before Renata could protest, Ernest was out of the car and

jogging back to the Denfert-Rochereau. Gunshots shattered the morning silence. Lights flickered on in apartments overlooking the plaza. A woman screamed. Ernest ducked behind a row of parked cars at the corner of the rue Froidevaux.

Across the plaza, the Bolshevik with the fake ear was sprawled on the sidewalk. His sidekick was crouched behind Beria's car. Beria had opened his door, using it for cover as he fired through the open window.

On the other side of the plaza, Goering and one of his men were huddled behind the kiosk near the metro station. Two Nazis lay writhing on the street, their blood staining the snow.

There was a momentary ceasefire. Ernest could see Goering talking to his man, instructing him, gesturing first toward the Bolsheviks, then toward a one-story brick building Ernest thought was a public bath. The Nazi reloaded his weapon, then started firing across the plaza.

On the ground next to Goering was the suitcase. Ernest leaned forward, trying to get a better look. Christ, thought Ernest, it *is* my case. The son of a bitch has my manuscripts with him.

Goering, suitcase in hand, sprinted across the street, taking his revolver out as he ran toward the bath house. Clumps of snow flew into the air near his feet, but the Bolsheviks failed to hit him.

Goering reached the bath house door, jammed his gun against the lock and fired. Then he kicked the door open and disappeared into the building.

Ernest took off after him.

The Nazi behind the kiosk spotted Ernest and took aim. As he pressed the trigger, Beria fired and the German's head exploded in a burst of blood.

Ernest stepped into the building. It was dark, lit only by the flame of a torch jutting from the wall about thirty feet away. Ernest inched down the corridor. He removed the torch, painfully aware that he was a clear target.

He reached a spiral staircase. Peering over the railing, he could see that the descent was lit by torches. Starting down the stairs, he wondered where the hell he was. One thing was certain: it was not a public bath house.

He counted more than ninety steps before his feet lighted

on a dirt-covered floor. A long, rocky cavern stretched out before him, torches spaced along the limestone walls.

He'd gone about a hundred yards when he heard something move up ahead. Flattening himself against the wall, he inched forward until he reached an open doorway on his right. Holding his breath, he waited for some movement, some sound. Nothing more. He shoved the torch through the doorway, illuminating a small, nearly empty room, its only inhabitant a large rat gnawing on a yellowed bone. The rat, its eyes glowing red in the light, scurried away. Ernest resumed his exploration.

From time to time, the corridor branched out into other byways, but Ernest kept to the main, torch-lit artery, each step making him more curious. Where the hell was he?

He got his answer a minute later.

Standing before an iron gate, he raised the torch in order to read an inscription on a plaque overhead.

"*Arrête, c'est ici l'empire de la mort.*"

The empire of the dead! He was at the entrance to the Paris catacombs.

He swung open the gate and walked in. Tens of thousands of blackened skulls were arranged in neat, shoulder-high piles, like so much firewood, the flickering light from the torch dipping in and out of the eyeless sockets, creating the illusion that the skulls were blinking.

The catacombs were mazelike; every thirty paces, another corridor appeared, or a doorway opened up on a chamber filled with more skulls, more bones. Ernest plowed on, sticking to the major cavern.

Everywhere he looked were reminders of his own mortality; in some spots, the skulls were arranged in special designs—a cross, a chalice, even an angel.

Nowhere, however, was there a sign of Goering.

Ernest's torch was dying. Dropping it to the ground, he reached for another torch on the wall. As he did, a gunshot ripped through the catacombs. A piece of limestone near his face blew away.

At the end of the corridor stood Goering, legs spread apart, pistol raised for a second shot.

Ernest dove to the floor. Two more shots flashed down the cavern. Ernest crawled behind a stack of bones shaped into a pyramid. Bullets splintered the skulls. The gunshots stopped. Ernest peered down the corridor. Goering was gone.

Ernest rolled across the ground, stood and grabbed a torch. The smell of gunpowder filled the corridor. He headed straight, moving cautiously in case Goering was waiting.

He'd gone about fifty yards when he reached a juncture divided into three branches. He swept the torch inches above the dirt floor, searching for footprints. Goering had obviously thought of the same thing—the entrances to all the caverns were stomped down, footprints going off in every direction.

He chose the left corridor and went less than a hundred feet before hitting a dead end. Cursing, he retraced his steps and returned to the juncture, this time taking the middle cavern.

There were no skulls in this corridor, but torches on the wall lit the way. The path looped to the right. As he turned, Ernest heard a moan, then another.

His back against the wall to make a smaller target, he continued ahead, coming to a wooden door on his left. Through a peephole, he spied a primitive wooden bed and a straightback chair. He opened the door. There was no one inside.

There was another moan, apparently from a second chamber down the cavern. Ernest stopped before the door. There was no peephole. He was certain this was the room he'd been brought to by the Nazis. The door creaked as he pressed his shoulder against the rotting wood. A man lay in the corner on a blanket, holding his stomach, moving back and forth in pain. It was the man Sergei had shot outside the Rotonde.

Ernest knelt beside the man, whose hands were covered with blood. The man's face was a death mask: ashen white, the features locked in a grimace of agony. He would soon die.

"Where's Goering?" asked Ernest in German, trying to make the words sound as though he were speaking his native tongue.

The man opened his eyes. Ernest lowered the torch so his face was lost in the shadows. "Is that you, Dietrich?" asked the man. "Have you brought a doctor?"

"Yes."

The man relaxed for a moment, then convulsed in pain, his bloody hand gripping Ernest's arm. "It hurts. It hurts."

"Where's Goering?"

"Gone. He . . . he took the woman."

"Where?"

Another spasm racked the man's body. "Where's the doctor? I need a doctor."

"He's coming," said Ernest. "Tell me where Goering went." The exchange was testing his rudimentary German.

"To the airfield. To . . . Le Bourget."

"I'll get a doctor," said Ernest, planning to call from the Montanais.

But the man's arm fell to his side and a rasping breath escaped from his parched lips. He was dead.

Ernest pulled the blanket over the man's face. Then he ran out of the room and followed the cavern until he reached a staircase, which he quickly ascended. At the top of the stairs were two doors: one, he figured, led to the Montanais. The other opened onto the alleyway.

He took the second. As expected, he found himself outside the bordello.

He went immediately to the garage. The tarpaulin lay on the floor. Unless Renata and Sergei had had some luck, Goering had escaped in Burchardt's Rolls-Royce.

And he still had Anastasia.

CHAPTER 22

Renata and Sergei had had no luck—the Austin was parked outside the Montanais when Ernest walked out of the alley.

"Did you see your father's Rolls come out of here?" asked Ernest as he climbed into the back seat.

"We just pulled up," said Renata. "One of the streets was blocked by a car accident and we had to make a detour."

"Goering's on his way to Le Bourget airfield with Anastasia. He has your father's car. He also has her documents and my manuscripts." Ernest took out Kurdorf's street guide and charted a course out of the city. "Tell Sergei to turn around. Le Bourget is north and we can take Raspail part of the way."

As they drove through the snow-laden streets of Paris, Ernest recounted his journey through the catacombs and his discovery of the dying Nazi.

"What happened to him after he told you about Goering?" asked Renata.

"He died."

Renata translated for Sergei, who nodded but showed no emotion at the news that the man he'd shot was dead.

They were out of Paris now, speeding through Aubervilliers, the huge chimneys from the factories the only structures free of snow. Ernest wondered how long ago the Rolls had passed; the snow on the road ahead was stamped with fresh tire tracks.

"Does Goering have a plane?" asked Ernest.

"I don't know," Renata said. "It's possible—he can certainly fly one. He was a hero during the war."

"So people keep telling me," said Ernest. "But I've never heard of him."

"Do you think we learned about American and British heroes? I assure you we didn't."

Ernest shrugged. He was tired, overwhelmed by the desire to sleep. He rubbed his eyes and stifled a yawn. Watching the snowy countryside glisten under the early morning sun, he thought about the past thirty-six hours: the news of the stolen manuscripts, the return to Paris, Renata, the ransacked apartment, the flight across the roof tops, the capture by the Nazis, the escape, the fight along the quai, making love to Renata, the gunfight outside the Rotonde, the chase through the catacombs.

He shook his head in disbelief. Who would ever believe such a tale? Would he ever dare to tell anyone?

"How much farther?" asked Renata.

Ernest looked out the window. They were passing a forest on the right, the tall firs frosted with snow, an army of shimmering Christmas trees. He waited until he saw a cottage in a clearing that he used as a landmark whenever he came out to Le Bourget. "We'll be there in a few minutes," he said.

The Austin jolted over a rise in the road. Ernest's hand brushed against his coat pocket. He felt the butt of Villwahr's pistol. Removing the gun from his pocket, he laid the weapon next to him on the seat.

"Don't you think you might need that?" asked Renata.

Ernest shook his head. "Not reliable."

The forest stopped at the foot of a steep hill. "Tell him to keep going—the airfield is just over the rise."

The Austin groaned and bucked as it worked its way up the hill. "All right," said Ernest when the car reached the top. "Just take it easy on the way down."

Sergei braked and the Austin slid down the hill. Flat countryside stretched before them to the horizon. They drove until a fork in the road appeared. "Bear to the left," said Ernest. "The road will take us right into Le Bourget."

A quarter of a mile later, the hangars came into view, their sloping tin roofs nearly buckling under the weight of the snowstorm. As they passed the last hangar, they saw the Rolls-Royce, its doors flung open, abandoned.

Two bedraggled workers were walking back to the main hangar, their shovels resting on their shoulders. They had just cleared away part of the runway; two hundred yards of rutted, frozen ground cut a brown swath through the snow-bound air strip. At the end of the runway was a red and black plane, its propellers whipping up clouds of snow.

"There they are!" screamed Renata, pointing through the windshield.

Ernest leaned forward. He could see Anastasia struggling fiercely as Goering tried to force her into the plane. She kicked and clawed at him as he dragged her, his right hand holding on to the briefcase—the briefcase that held the Romanov documents and his manuscripts.

Sergei floored the Austin, steering for the runway. The car hit a patch of ice. Sergei twisted the steering wheel as the car swerved nearly ninety degrees, then tilted on its two right wheels. Ernest grabbed the door handle and tried to prop himself up, hoping his weight would force the car down on all four wheels. But before he could, the Austin turned over on the driver side.

Glass shattered. Renata screamed. Ernest dug his heels into the back of the front seat. Sergei's head smashed against the steering wheel as the car came to a crunching stop.

Blood poured down Sergei's face. Ernest reached down and shook the unconscious Sergei by the shoulders, trying to revive him. The Russian didn't move. Ernest fished through Sergei's coat. Grabbing Sergei's revolver, he pushed open the side door and pulled himself out of the wreckage, jumping to the ground.

The plane was coming down the runway.

Renata began to make her way out of the car.

Ernest ran until he reached the side of the runway. Then he knelt down, raised the gun towards the plane and waited. He could see Goering in the front cockpit, could see that the rear compartment was empty. The plane lifted off the ground.

Ernest pumped off six shots, emptying the revolver, knowing that a handgun was unlikely to damage the plane or hit Goering.

He wasn't surprised when the plane picked up altitude until it was a mere speck in the morning sky. He dropped the gun, cursing under his breath.

Goering had escaped.

Goering had won.

Or had he?

Someone was hugging the ground near the end of the runway.

As Ernest neared the figure, he realized Goering hadn't won anything. He no longer had Anastasia.

She was kneeling now, watching Ernest approach, watching him warily, as if at any moment she would run away.

Sensing her fear, her confusion, he stopped a few feet short. "I'm a friend," he said in French. "I'm here to help you."

She stared at him as if she didn't understand his words. Dark rings circled her eyes, thin red lines scarred her neck. She looked nothing like a Grand Duchess of the Romanov Empire.

Ernest moved closer, extending his right hand, expecting her to bolt. She didn't move. He was about to help her up when Renata yelled across the runway.

"Get away from her!"

Ernest turned. Renata was standing in the middle of the runway, about thirty feet away. A gun held in her right hand was aimed at him.

"Get away," she said.

"What the hell are you talking about?"

"Move away from her. I don't want to kill both of you."

"Both of us? Are you crazy? This is Anastasia, this is the woman you've been trying to rescue."

A cold, triumphant smile flashed across Renata's face. "She's not Anastasia—I am."

"Bullshit."

The woman behind him began to whimper.

"I told you to move away."

"If you're Anastasia, who the hell is this?"

"Her name is Anna Aronson. She's a Russian peasant who worked as a maid for Nicholas Burchardt. She is mentally unstable. She stole my documents and came to Paris. She claimed she was me. She had the documents. She even had scars."

"Scars? So what?"

"The real Anastasia has scars from the night she survived the Bolshevik assassination squad. I don't know how that impostor got hers."

"But you don't—"

"I do. Many of them. That's why I turned the lights off last night. So you wouldn't see them. So you wouldn't ask questions."

Ernest now had no doubts that she was telling the truth; she no longer had any reason to lie. He'd been a fool and there was no one to blame but himself.

"You're worse than a whore," he said. "You've been lying all along, faking everything."

"Not everything," she said. "Not last night."

"Drop the act—the play's over."

"Not quite. Move away."

Anna got to her feet and stood directly behind Ernest.

"Why does she have to die?" he asked.

"Walk away, Ernest. This isn't your affair."

"Like hell it isn't," he said. "Answer me! Why must she die?"

"Because I need time. The Bolsheviks want me dead. The Whites want me to lead them. But there are many traitors in the White movement. The moment I agree to unite their cause, I'll be assassinated. I need time to find my own people, people I can trust. I need time to perfect a plan not just to unite the Whites but to lead them victoriously back to Russia."

"So you have to kill Anna?"

"Don't you understand? No one outside the Burchardt household knows the truth, knows that she is not genuine. The Bolsheviks and Whites will stop hunting me if they think I'm dead. I'll be free to go about my work. There's no choice—she has to die."

Ernest stood his ground.

"I don't want to kill you. But I will," she said, walking toward him.

A plane was coming into the field behind her, its nose pointing down as it angled for the runway.

Anastasia kept walking. She was only five feet away when Ernest recognized the gun she was holding. It was the useless pistol he'd taken off the suicidal Frenchman.

The plane was almost over the runway. Anastasia glanced over her shoulder. Ernest lunged. She pulled the trigger.

This time the gun worked.

Momentarily distracted by the incoming plane, Anastasia's aim was off. The bullet sliced through one side of Ernest's billowing coat.

Ernest tackled her to the ground. The gun jostled from her hand. The plane did not land, but flew directly over them, only ten feet above the runway. It was a red and black plane. Goering's plane.

The plane banked and turned, closing in on them. A fiery ball fell from the plane onto the runway. The plane swooped over them, then disappeared into the bright eastern sky.

Anastasia struggled to free herself from Ernest's grip. Standing, he dragged her towards the fire. The smell of brandy filled the air; whatever was burning had been doused with liquor to assure an efficient blaze.

It had worked; whatever was burning was now totally consumed by flame. Keeping a firm hold on her arm, Ernest allowed Anastasia to stand. Together, they approached the fire.

Ernest immediately recognized part of his suitcase in the flame. Only the small section of the case with his initials and the tarnished belt buckle remained.

Everything else—the Romanov documents, his manuscripts—was ashes.

Goering, presumably concluding that his mission was a failure, must have decided to extract the final revenge and destroy the documents and manuscripts, Ernest thought.

Ernest made no move to scavenge through the ashes. There was nothing to salvage. Goering had won after all.

Anastasia cried out and desperately, pathetically, began throwing handfuls of snow on the fire. But it was too late. As the fire died, she sifted through the charred remains, finding only the blackened cover of a Bible.

She was crying.

"Tough break," said Ernest.

Standing up, she attempted to dry her tears. "I still have half my papers."

"But that only makes you half credible." He walked over to Anna Aronson and led her down the runway.

Anastasia called his name twice, then broke down, kneeling beside the ashes, sobbing.

Ernest kept walking. He no longer cared.

Sitting in his study, Leo Nelson finished reading the last of the Hemingway stories Offenbach had sold him. There were fourteen stories, two dozen poems and part of a novel. The poems and novel didn't interest him; he didn't write poetry and he was perceptive enough to realize that the novel was a very rough first draft.

But the stories, damn it. The stories were good. Nelson was stunned that someone as young as Hemingway could have mastered such a powerful, distinctive style. Hemingway was going to be a great writer.

Nelson's anger burned within him. Why Hemingway and not me? It wasn't fair.

He pondered what he should do with the manuscripts. He could always return them to Hemingway. Hemingway would make a valuable friend. But Hemingway despised him.

And he despised Hemingway. He recalled the scene in the Amateurs, when Hemingway had humiliated him in front of Clive Russet.

No, he would not give the manuscripts back.

Nelson looked at the pile of manuscripts, carbons and notebooks on his desk. Suddenly, he didn't want any of it. They reminded him too much of his own failure.

He knew what to do.

Opening a desk drawer, he took out a pair of scissors. Then, slowly, methodically, he picked up a page from a short story and began to cut the paper in half, then quarters, then eighths.

For the next hour he shredded every page of every short story, every poem, every chapter of the novel in progress. When he was done, he brushed the slips of paper into a manila envelope and walked out on the balcony off his study.

The apartment was on the rue Saint-Paul, overlooking the Seine. He waited until a strong wind gusted down the river. Then he opened the envelope and shook the confettilike bits into the air.

Some glided to the snow below the balcony. But most were carried to the river, settling on the water like so many falling leaves.

He watched the river carry them under the Pont Sully. Smiling, he walked back into his apartment.

CHAPTER 23

Ernest had about twenty minutes to kill before the ten P.M. train to Lausanne and points south departed. He bought a racing form at the newsstand in the Gare de Lyon, then settled comfortably at a table in the cafe near the station's entrance.

He ordered a sausage sandwich and a glass of beer. The sandwich was stale and he ate only half, saving the rest for the long train ride ahead. The beer tasted wonderful and he drank quickly and ordered another. He couldn't think of anyone in Paris who had a better reason for drinking.

It had been a hell of a day.

He'd driven Anna Aronson back to Paris in Burchardt's Rolls-Royce. She spoke little, but under questioning acknowledged that she had some friends in Berlin who would help her. She no longer seemed to be suffering from any delusion that she was Anastasia, and Ernest didn't press the point.

Once in Paris, he deposited her at Sylvia Beach's bookstore, then called James Joyce. Since Joyce was leaving that night for his surgery in Berlin, would he let a young woman accompany him and his wife? asked Ernest.

Joyce was kind enough to agree.

Ernest then went home and slept for five hours, a tossing, restless sleep despite his exhaustion. Famished when he awakened, he quickly dressed, packed his bag and went to a small but excellent restaurant around the corner. He ate a dozen oysters, a cold lobster, and a bottle of wine. He overtipped the waiter with his last francs.

He got to Shakespeare and Company a few minutes before closing time. Sylvia reported that Anna had been quiet all day, apparently content to just browse through the books.

Ernest told Sylvia about the Joyces, then sheepishly admitted that he was broke. Sylvia loaned him some cash and promised to look after the young woman until the Joyces came for her. Sylvia also said she would spring for Anna's train ticket.

"Pay me when you sell your first novel," Sylvia had told Ernest.

Next, he drove the Rolls to the rue Saint-Gilles and parked outside a monastery run by the Brothers of the Sacred Heart, an order that specialized in educational work in the poorest areas of the world. He slipped the keys to the limousine inside an envelope, which he dropped into the mail slot in the front door. Inside the envelope was an unsigned note turning the car over to the brothers on the condition that they sell the Rolls and use the proceeds for their missions.

At least something good had come of the Romanov affair.

So now he was sitting in the Gare de Lyon, finishing his second beer, considering a third, and waiting for the train that would take him back to Lausanne, back to journalism, back to Hadley.

He didn't mind going back to any of them. The journalism, he knew, was a temporary thing. He had decided to turn down the job offer with Allied News. He was going to write fiction, the best ever written; his search for the stolen manuscripts only proved to him how much a career as a writer—not a reporter—meant to him. He would rewrite those stories. It would be a bitch of a job but he'd do it. And he'd make them better.

One reason he'd make them better was Hadley. He loved her and she deserved a hell of a lot more than a four-story walk-up in the Latin Quarter. It might take a year or two but he'd write his way out. He'd do it because he'd have Hadley with him.

Against his wishes, he thought then of Renata, or rather, Anastasia. During the ride back to Paris, Anna had confirmed that the woman they'd left at Le Bourget was, indeed, the daughter of the Czar.

Which meant that he'd made love to a Grand Duchess.

Big deal.

He'd also been betrayed by a Grand Duchess, taken for one hell of a ride. It would never happen again. But . . . but the memory of Anastasia lingered despite the lies, despite the deceit. He'd been a fool. But what man would not have been in his place? He would never forget her. Deciding against another beer, he walked out of the cafe and headed for his train.

Anastasia was waiting for him at the gate.

"I thought you might be going back to Lausanne," she said. She was dressed exactly the same way as she'd been on the *Orient Express*. Ernest wondered why she was here; there were too many people in the station for her to risk killing him.

"I have a train to catch," he said, brushing past her.

She walked along. "I wanted to say how sorry I was."

Ernest stopped. "Why don't you get the hell out of here?"

"I want you to understand—I didn't know what I was doing this morning," she said, her voice trembling.

Ernest laughed. "Bullshit."

"And I wanted to tell you that Sergei will be all right. He'll be in the hospital for some time but he'll recover."

"I'll have to send him a get-well card."

She put her hand on his arm. "I want to see you again. Not everything I did with you was playacting."

"Forget it," said Ernest, jerking his arm away.

"But—"

Ernest turned and walked towards the train.

"Wait, Ernest. Please," she said, running after him. "I need you. Please stay."

He didn't look back. Nodding to the conductor at the gate, he walked to the train and climbed aboard.

He found an empty compartment, pulled down the window shades and sat down, resting his legs on the opposite seat. Praying he'd have no companions, he closed his eyes and began to doze, only to be rudely awakened a minute later by someone loudly sliding open the door to the compartment.

"Fancy meeting you here," said a female voice.

Ernest opened his eyes to see Sara Morgan standing in the doorway. "What the hell are you—"

"Don't ask," said Sara, hefting her suitcase onto the luggage rack and sitting next to him.

"I'm asking," said Ernest. "The last time I saw you you were in Lausanne."

"I was. In fact, I was in the hotel room of a very handsome Greek gentleman—interviewing him, of course—when I got a call from our London office. They'd heard a rumor about some activity in Paris involving some Russians, some Germans and—get this—the daughter of the Czar."

"You're kidding."

"I wish I was. They sent me back to Paris on the next train to try to track down the story."

"Did you?"

"A wild goose chase. Nothing."

Ernest tried to keep a straight face. He failed.

"What the hell's so funny?" she asked over his laughter.

"You wouldn't believe me."

"Try me."

The train moved out of the station. Ernest stopped chuckling and studied Sara, wondering if he could trust her. He had to tell someone, had to get the whole mess off his chest.

"If I tell you, you have to swear that you'll never repeat a word of what I say. Never."

Sara crossed her heart like a schoolgirl. "I promise."

"All right," said Ernest. "Sit back—it's a long story."

For the next hour, he told her everything—from the theft of the manuscripts to his final confrontation with Anastasia.

"My God," said Sara when he was done. "That's fantastic."

"I know."

"You've got to write a book about it. You can make a bundle."

Ernest shook his head.

"Why not?" demanded Sara. "It would be incredible. You'd have publishers crawling all over you to get their hands on it."

"Probably. But I'm not interested."

"Why the hell not?" she asked.

Ernest stared out the window as the train swept through Dijon. Sara lit a cigarette.

"I want to know, Ernest, why you're not going to turn that tale into a book."

Ernest looked at her and smiled. "I don't want to write a potboiler."

WHO WAS SARA MORGAN?

Born in Rhinebeck, New York, in 1897, SARA MORGAN became a newspaper reporter when she was just twenty years old. For the next several years, she covered major stories around the world: America's entry into World War I and the fall of Germany; the Black Sox baseball scandal of 1919; postwar Europe; Prohibition; the St. Valentine's Day Massacre and the Lindbergh kidnapping. In 1930, she herself made headlines when she single-handedly recovered the fabled Emerald of Osiris, which had been stolen while on tour in America by members of the powerful Palagonia gang from Detroit. She left the newspaper business to write novels, which led to a long and profitable career scripting movies. An unfriendly witness before the House Committee on Un-American Activities in 1950, she was blacklisted. She moved to Carmel, California, where she wrote an occasional mystery and waged a vigorous campaign to safeguard the large otter community at nearby Point Lobos. Sara Morgan died in 1982.

ABOUT THE AUTHOR

VINCENT COSGROVE's life has been nowhere as exciting as Sara Morgan's. A reporter for the New York *Daily News*, he lives in Staten Island with his wife and daughter and is working on a new novel.

THE WORLD FANTASY AWARD-WINNING NOVEL

"AMBITIOUS, DAZZLING, STRANGELY MOVING, A MARVELOUS MAGIC-REALIST FAMILY CHRONICLE."
—*Book World (The Washington Post)*

Little, Big
by John Crowley

Somewhere beyond the city, at the edge of a wildwood, sits a house on the border between reality and fantasy, a place where the lives of faeries and mortals intertwine. Sometime in our age, a young man in love comes here to be wed, and enters a family whose Tale reaches backward and forward a hundred years, from the sunlit hours of a gentler time, to the last, dark days of this century—and beyond to a new dawn.

Sensual, exuberant, witty, and wise, LITTLE, BIG is a true masterpiece, a tale of wonder you will take to your heart and treasure for years to come. It is on sale September 15, 1983, wherever Bantam paperbacks are sold, or you can use this handy coupon for ordering:

Bantam Books, Inc., Dept. LB1, 414 East Golf Road, Des Plaines, Ill. 60016

Please send me _____ copies of LITTLE, BIG (23337-8 • $3.95). I am enclosing $ _____ (please add $1.25 to cover postage and handling. Send check or money order—no cash or C.O.D.'s please).

Mr/Ms _____
Address _____
City/State _____ Zip _____

LB1—9/83
Please allow four to six weeks for delivery. This offer expires 3/84.

DON'T MISS
THESE CURRENT
Bantam Bestsellers

☐	23481	**THE VALLEY OF HORSES** Jean M. Auel	$4.50
☐	23670	**WHAT ABOUT THE BABY?** Clare McNally	$2.95
☐	22775	**CLAN OF THE CAVE BEAR** Jean M. Auel	$3.95
☐	23302	**WORLDLY GOODS** Michael Korda	$3.95
☐	23353	**MADONNA RED** James Carroll	$3.95
☐	23105	**NO COMEBACKS** F. Forsyth	$3.50
☐	23291	**JERICHO** A. Costello	$3.95
☐	23187	**THE TOMBSTONE CIPHER** Ib Melchoir	$3.50
☐	22929	**SCORPION EAST** J. Morgulas	$3.50
☐	22926	**ROCKABYE** Laird Koenig	$3.25
☐	22913	**HARLEQUIN** Morris West	$3.50
☐	22838	**TRADITIONS** Alan Ebert w/ Janice Rotchstein	$3.95
☐	22866	**PACIFIC VORTEX** Clive Cussler	$3.95
☐	22520	**GHOST LIGHT** Clare McNally	$2.95
☐	22656	**NO TIME FOR TEARS** Cynthia Freeman	$3.95
☐	22580	**PEACE BREAKS OUT** John Knowles	$2.95
☐	20922	**SHADOW OF CAIN** Vincent Bugliosi & Ken Hurwitz	$3.95
☐	20822	**THE GLITTER DOME** Joseph Wambaugh	$3.95
☐	20924	**THE PEOPLE'S ALMANAC 3** Wallechinsky & Wallace	$4.50
☐	20662	**THE CLOWNS OF GOD** Morris West	$3.95
☐	20181	**CHALLENGE (Spirit of America!)** Charles Whited	$3.50

Prices and availability subject to change without notice.

Buy them at your local bookstore or use this handy coupon for ordering:

Bantam Books, Inc., Dept. FB, 414 East Golf Road, Des Plaines, Ill. 60016

Please send me the books I have checked above. I am enclosing $_____ (please add $1.25 to cover postage and handling). Send check or money order —no cash or C.O.D.'s please.

Mr/Mrs/Miss_____

Address_____

City_____ State/Zip_____

FB—9/83

Please allow four to six weeks for delivery. This offer expires 3/84.

RELAX!
SIT DOWN
and Catch Up On Your Reading!

☐	05034	BALE FIRE by Ken Goddard (Hardcover)	$14.95
☐	23678	WOLFSBANE by Craig Thomas	$3.95
☐	23420	THE CIRCLE by Steve Shagan	$3.95
☐	23567	SAVE THE TIGER by Steve Shagan	$3.25
☐	23483	THE CROOKED ROAD by Morris West	$2.95
☐	22913	HARLEQUIN by Morris West	$3.50
☐	20694	DAUGHTER OF SILENCE by Morris West	$2.95
☐	22746	RED DRAGON by Thomas Harris	$3.95
☐	23838	SEA LEOPARD by Craig Thomas	$3.95
☐	20353	MURDER AT THE RED OCTOBER by Anthony Olcott	$2.95
☐	20662	CLOWNS OF GOD by Morris West	$3.95
☐	20688	TOWER OF BABEL by Morris West	$3.50
☐	22812	THE BOURNE IDENTITY by Robert Ludlum	$3.95
☐	20879	THE CHANCELLOR MANUSCRIPT by Robert Ludlum	$3.95
☐	20720	THE MATARESE CIRCLE by Robert Ludlum	$3.95
☐	23149	SMILEY'S PEOPLE by John Le Carre	$3.95
☐	23159	THE DEVIL'S ALTERNATIVE by Frederick Forsyth	$3.95
☐	13801	THE FORMULA by Steve Shagan	$2.75
☐	22787	STORM WARNING by Jack Higgins	$3.50
☐	23781	SNOW FALCON by Craig Thomas	$3.95
☐	22709	FIREFOX by Craig Thomas	$3.50

Prices and availability subject to change without notice.

Buy them at your local bookstore or use this handy coupon for ordering:

Bantam Books, Inc., Dept. FBB, 414 East Golf Road, Des Plaines, III. 60016

Please send me the books I have checked above. I am enclosing $_____
(please add $1.25 to cover postage and handling). Send check or money order
—no cash or C.O.D.'s please.

Mr/Mrs/Miss_____

Address _____

City_____ State/Zip_____

FBB—10/83
Please allow four to six weeks for delivery. This offer expires 4/84.